PRAISE FOR *STORYTELLING, WISDOM, AND ARCHETYPES*

Dr. Annabelle Nelson shows us the amazing power of storytelling in transforming consciousness to cultivate both spiritual awareness and emotional stability. We learn how stories from around the world are an ancient human technology for passing on culture and wisdom. Dr. Nelson has worked with stories for over twenty years to help others create maps for facing adversity and the challenges of daily life. Through her writing, we learn how to use storytelling in our lives to gain perspective, clarity, and direction—and even wisdom. She assures us that if we intend to grow into our potential, we are all capable of becoming wise through the practice of calmly focusing the mind, without a goal of becoming something else, but with the intention of becoming oneself.

-Stephen Murphy-Shigematsu, EdD
professor, Stanford School of Medicine
and author of *From Mindfulness to Heartfulness:
Transforming Self and Society with Compassion*

Dr. Annabelle Nelson's brilliant work invites us to literally restory our psyches and consciousness to enter our fuller human potential. I have followed Nelson's work for years, and this book is incredibly poignant and accessible, teaching the reader how entering the realm of story through the archetypal is a path to fullness and wisdom.

-Jeanine M. Canty, PhD
professor, California Institute of Integral Studies,
author of *Returning the Self to Nature: Undoing Our
Collective Narcissism and Healing the Planet*

Storytelling, Wisdom, and Archetypes

Storytelling, Wisdom, and Archetypes

Why Stories Matter—
and How They Shape Our Lives

Annabelle Nelson

MANDORLA BOOKS

DEDICATION

To three inspirational, cutting-edge women: Jeanne Achterberg, the imagery shaman; Marion Woodman, the archetype maven; and Mary Elizabeth McCoy Nelson, my storyteller

TABLE OF CONTENTS

Prologue..1

    Why This Book: Storytelling, Wisdom, and Archetypes............9

    The Wise Mind-Body Model...12

    The Stories in This Book..15

Chapter One: The Journey..**21**

    My Journey..24

    Yoga: Focus the Mind...25

    Imagery: Focusing the Mind and Transforming Emotions.......36

    Archetypes: Archetypal Identification Transforms Emotions...48

    Storytelling: Bringing It Together....................................51

Chapter Two: Wisdom...**55**

    Wisdom Is Going Beyond and Through................................55

    Wisdom Is Emotional Balance..61

    Wisdom Is Spiritual..64

    Wisdom Is Creative...66

    Wisdom Is Paradoxical...67

    Wisdom Is Inter-individual..70

    Qualities of Wisdom...72

Chapter Three: Storytelling..**75**

    Wheels for Balance and Harmony.....................................78

    Stories for Balance and Harmony.....................................84

    Stories' Purposes...87

Creating a Story...91

Another Way to Create a Story 94

Chapter Four: Storytelling Archetypes....................97

Story Characters and Archetypes 97

Storytelling & Archetypal Identification.........................99

Finding an Archetype, Creating a Story 103

Finding an Archetype 108

Chapter Five: The Storytelling Cycle....................109

Campbell's Stages of the Hero's Journey 110

Examples of the Stages 111

Resiliency in the Return 117

Stories Are Transformational 123

Storytelling and Expanded Consciousness........................126

Chapter Six: The Storytelling Virtues...................127

The Storytelling Five Virtues 127

Storytelling Virtue: Acceptance 128

Storytelling Virtue: Tests 129

Storytelling Virtue: Bravery 130

Storytelling Virtue: Beauty 132

Storytelling Virtue: Death/Rebirth 133

Chapter Seven: The Virtue of Acceptance.................135

Ganesha 135

The Children..137

Avalokiteśvara..138

Chapter Eight: The Virtue of Tests 141

Ramayana 141

Keep on Steppin' 144

The Dragon's Robe 146

The Four Directions 149

Sophia and Claude 152

Post-Traumatic Growth 157

Chapter Nine: The Virtue of Bravery **161**

Juan Bobo 161

Lilith 163

La Llorona 164

Isis 165

Gaia 166

Buffalo Woman 167

Chapter Ten: The Virtue of Beauty **171**

Ganesha 171

The White Spider 173

Coyote and His Pups 176

Chapter Eleven: The Virtue of Death and Rebirth **181**

John the True 181

Deirdre 186

Chapter Twelve: The Storytelling Five **189**

Storytelling Virtues Helix 189

The Shaman Story 190

Xenophobe 193

Cupid and Psyche 196

Coyote and the Cottontail: Cotton Tail Cheats Death 200

Epilogue: Life as Story **203**

Visualize the Beginning 206

Think About the Return...206

Tell Your Story...207

A Note about References and Cultural Competency & Humility...**209**

Format for References and Citations.................................209

Cultural Competence and Cultural Humility 209

Sources for the Book's Stories 210

Bibliography **213**

Prologue

To become wise, a person needs both spiritual awareness and emotional strength. At first glance, it might seem far-fetched that storytelling can catalyze these changes. On reflection, though, it makes sense. Stories are ancient human technology passed down orally from elder to child, transmitting the collective wisdom of human experience. Stories tell people where they came from and where they are going. Metaphoric in nature, stories talk to the deep levels of unconscious knowing. When people listen to or tell stories, they are relaxed. As an example of this relaxation power, think of a three-year-old being read a story at night: the face relaxes, the jaw unclenches, and the eyes soften. These ancestral response patterns reside in adults as well. In addition to relaxing the mind, stories create pictures. When one listens to a good story, it is almost like a movie unfolding. The story's characters are archetypal in nature, embodying patterns and skills for solving life's problems.

People visualize the character's feats in their minds, creating a visual focus which psychologists call *visual imagery*. Research on imagery shows that thinking in pictures engages the memory centers in the brain, opening and naturally releasing emotional material. The mind becomes more spacious and clearer. Paradoxically, not only the content of stories but also the process of listening and telling stories brings awareness and inner stability. In the following chapters, I will detail how storytelling can transform consciousness to cultivate both spiritual awareness and emotional stability.

In his book *The Heart of the Buddha*, Chögyam Trungpa, a Tibetan Buddhist teacher, gives a practical example of what it means to be wise. Trungpa says that if a person is wise, then they have friendliness and warmth for themselves and for the whole world. They have a calm center that allows perceptions to come and go and allows emotions to be released as the clouds float in the sky. This might strike a reader as counterintuitive: that wisdom is characterized by friendliness to oneself and others.

But a relaxed, calm inner state is wisdom. The inner world is transformed.

People define wisdom in a number of ways. For example, some scholars report that wisdom is the balance of knowledge and experience complemented by moral sensibilities. Some people say it is a state of enlightenment or transcendence marked by altruism. Others say only a few humans can become wise. However, I don't think it is what people know or what they have experienced. Rather, it is a transcendent state of consciousness.

My take on wisdom is that all humans can become wise. It requires the intention to grow into one's potential. It also requires practice to calmly focus the mind, without a goal of becoming something else, but with the intention of becoming oneself.

Focused practice creates an inner awareness that is not overwhelmed by incoming perceptions or eruptions from unconscious patterns or emotions, such as worry or anxiety. It's not like the person is a yogi in a cave in the Himalayas, sitting in full lotus, emotionless. It is creating awareness. As the great yogi Patanjali says in the *Yoga Sutras,* as reported by Edwin Bryant, a transformed mind is like the sky—the clouds, and even storms pass through, but they don't stay. Just like the sky, a transformed mind allows flow and gives space for inner potential to have its play. A focus of attention transforms the mind over time. Emotions pass through, insights emerge, rational thoughts conclude, experience reflects, worries dissipate, and creativity paints ideas. Further, the focus allows the mind to relax and unwind, even allowing hidden emotions and repressed storylines to move up and out of the unconscious.

I came to this definition of wisdom through many years of studying psychology, imagery, brain physiology, Buddhist and Hindu philosophy, and also practicing yoga and meditation. But the seed for this definition was planted when I was a young graduate student in psychology at the University of Kansas. I was part of a committee that brought speakers to campus. I discovered Elmer Green, a bi-opsychologist, at the nearby Menninger Clinic, a famous Freudian clinic, in Topeka, Kansas. He was studying yogis in India and taking physiological data as the yogis stopped their hearts. I was fascinated. Even though I was studying behavioral psychology, a discipline that didn't admit there was human potential other than rational thoughts, I was struck by Green's presentation of the potential of the mind discovered by studying yogis. I was open to his ideas since I had started doing yoga to deal with the stress of graduate school and had noticed major effects in my ability to be calm.

When I walked into the auditorium, Dr. Green was projecting a transparency from an overhead projector on the screen. He said the ultimate goal of human development was for the conscious to become unconscious and the unconscious to become conscious. Something inside said, "Aha." I had an immediate knowing that was the metaphor for understanding how people could reach their potential.

I've often had the feeling that there is something outside of my consciousness. To me, my consciousness occupies a space radiating 360 degrees from the middle of my head, up above me, and down through my body. However, at times, I felt a space outside my awareness that I can't quite get to. That's why Green's image was so salient for me. Later, I studied Jungian psychology, reading A *Man and His Symbols*. Jung posits that there is a collective unconscious that unites humans but is usually not reachable in our day-to-day thought process. Jung reportedly said that either the unconscious runs a person, or the person runs their unconscious. The path to wisdom is to open the unconscious.

This is a tricky process since the conscious mind identifies with the ego. As Sigmund Freud said, the ego will fight tooth and nail to keep the unconscious from opening. But C.G. Jung taught that focusing on an archetype safely opens the unconscious. A natural and easy way to do this is to focus on one main character in a story. This character could be an archetype. Jung posited three main archetypes: anima (female), animus (male), and the shadow, what is unknown about the self. In my book, *Archetypal Imagery,* I define an archetype as an energy pattern in the collective unconscious that conveys a discernible and immediate characteristic. For example, Hercules may convey strength, or Marilyn Monroe may convey sexuality.

There is a lot going on inside the human being that is outside of conscious awareness. People think that they are actually the words running in their minds. But there is much more. It could be golden potential that is unknown, or memories, emotions, and storylines that trap energy. If the mind can be focused in a calm manner, then it can unwind naturally. Further, if one focuses on an image of an archetype, that can create a safe opening to memories. What I mean by a relaxed focus is that the person isn't trying to figure something out or achieve a goal, but the mind is focused on something, as in a word, a part of the body, a prayer, or an image of a character in a story. There isn't a goal but just a focus. This opens the unconscious, allowing material to be released and insights to emerge.

Opening the unconscious has four significant benefits.

1. It is relaxing.
2. Emotional material that is repressed can slowly unwind and be released.
3. The inner world becomes spacious, so perceptions can be clear, and both the rational and intuitive capabilities can be active.
4. It allows insights to emerge from the collective unconscious that are spiritual and creative in nature, prompting individuation and wisdom.

Practices that include focusing are meditation and yoga. It is a relaxed focus. It is not concentration like trying to figure out a problem; it is focusing on something that might even be nonsensical, like the repetition of a number, a mantra, or sensing part of the body in a yoga pose. Herbert Benson was a medical doctor and, in his 1976 book *The Relaxation Response*, he talks about repeating a number, such as "1, 1, 1, 1, 1." He had previously worked with Maharishi Mahesh Yogi, the teacher of Transcendental Meditation, who taught meditation to The Beatles. Instead of a Hindu mantra, Benson found that one could just repeat a number, and it had the same result. Benson talks about the need for what he calls a "passive attitude" as well. This means not concentrating, or using the focus to achieve a goal, but just to be.

Through my quest to find natural ways for people to unfold to their potential, I studied psychology in many different forms: humanistic, Jungian, behaviorism, the cognitive process of imagery, as well as the spiritual practices of yoga and meditation. I talked to experts, traveled internationally, and taught in India, among other things. When I was working on educational and health programs on the Tohono O'odham Nation in southern Arizona, I was struck by the power of storytelling. This rekindled my early memories of my mother telling stories. She was a drama and speech teacher at a high school and would tell stories at women's clubs. As I watched her dress in a big hat and a fake braid, holding a basket of flowers that embodied her stories, I was imprinted with the storytelling modality. After trying many methods to find a natural way for humans to become wise, I returned to this method from my childhood that my work with the Tohono O'odham catalyzed.

For the unconscious to become conscious, and vice versa, a relaxed state of consciousness is required. When the mind is relaxed, something happens to the consciousness. A space emerges that might be called *liminal*. Liminal comes from the Latin word *limen*, which translates as a threshold. It is a transitional space. A practice that passively focuses the mind opens this liminal space.

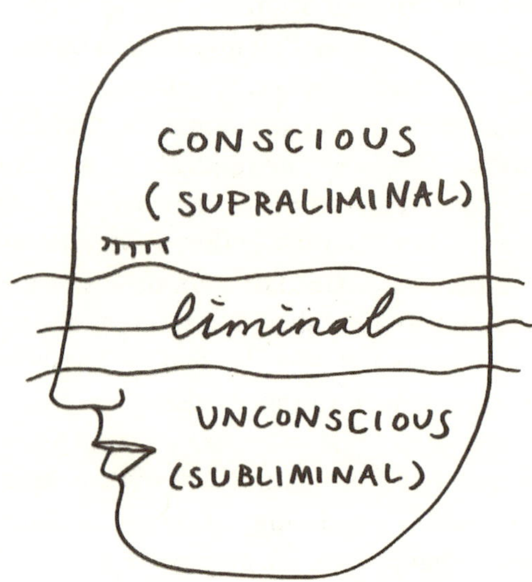

Liminal spaces open the mind to interconnections. In this state, a person experiences a shift in consciousness, perceiving reality as it is and sensing the streams of human wisdom laid down over the centuries. What I have found in my journey to move myself and others to wisdom is that storytelling is a natural way to evoke liminality—betwixt and between, both/and, neither/nor, undoing and unbinding.

Liminality is the space between one state and another that hastens the transformation of consciousness to wisdom. Folklorist Arnold van Gennep coined the term in his 1909 book *The Rites of Passage* after studying rituals. He examined initiation rituals in both individual and community events. Listening to stories creates a doorway or a passage to a space where centuries of human wisdom reside. Humans are born with a sense of story, and stories open up this critical consciousness. Liminal spaces are formative moments that allow a person to leap into the unknown, as defined by Paul Stenner in 2017. A solid structure melts into liquid when a story's hero or heroine has a call to adventure that changes life forever.

Stable ground shifts. Liminality creates formative moments of great significance.

One of my first memories of experiencing a liminal space, a threshold to an expanded state of awareness, was as a teenager in Kansas City, Missouri. Kansas City is known as the city of boulevards and fountains. I remember riding through the city late at night with my friends, my head hanging out the window, looking up. The wind was rustling the huge elm trees. This was before the Dutch elm disease cleaned them out. I looked up, enraptured by the sound of the leaves rustling, and the sight of the canopy made by the huge trees being spotlighted by streetlamps in a rhythmic sequence— timeless joy; time changed; experience, not thought.

Another vivid memory of experiencing liminal spaces was with a group several years ago. I taught courses in mysticism at Prescott College in Prescott, Arizona. It was, in part, based on shamanism. In my studies, I noticed that drumming created altered states of consciousness. This overlapped with my yoga practice and my studies of the cognitive process of imagery. Imagery is thinking in terms of internal sensations (such as sight, sound, movement, odors, touch, or taste) that communicate with the inner part of the brain, the limbic system. It's the part of the brain that expands perception and opens memory banks. In other words, thinking in pictures or in the cognitive process of imagery creates liminality.

In the mysticism class, I prompted students to find a spiritual path that they were attuned to, and we did improvisational drumming together. I often led the class in imagery before or after the drumming to create altered states of consciousness. Many things happened. The improvisational rhythm during class sessions prompted feelings of joy and interconnection with others as endorphins rained in our brains. Also, group intuition seemed to be alive. After we debriefed on the experience, a number of students reported they saw a tree growing in the middle of the circle of people. We had created a liminal space, a space outside of normal waking reality, a threshold, a doorway from one state to another. In the case of my class, the shift was from normal waking reality to a sense of interconnection and wonderment.

In my work on American Indian Nations in Arizona, I was fortunate to hear tribal leaders talk about story as the primary mode of learning. (American Indian, Indian, Native American, or Native are acceptable and often used interchangeably in the United States.) With my research on imagery, I knew that thinking in pictures could open the mind to expanded states of consciousness. When people think about stories, they see pictures in their minds when they hear a good one.

I started a nonprofit with some colleagues named the Wholistic Health Education and Empowerment for Life (WHEEL) Council. Our mission was to use storytelling, the arts, and cultural knowledge to help young people thrive. We had national conferences with the theme "stories heal." Storytellers from many cultures told stories, and liminal spaces emerged. Listeners' faces relaxed, their bodies became less rigid, their eyes opened, and their jaws unclenched, creating an opening to the inner world. Stories are often circular. The main character is challenged by a test and must seek helpers, both physical and spiritual, to navigate it and return in a new state. Stories' circularity mirrors the cyclic nature of life, fostering harmony with the natural world. As I was writing this book, I often felt that circularity. It didn't seem as if I was making progress, but rather that I was lost in the book. Over the years, as I worked on this book, I have often felt that I was in a liminal space. I hope that this happens for the reader moving through these pages, a little liminality to touch the wisdom inside.

The Storytelling Wisdom Psychodynamic

Storytelling is a perfect vehicle to transform consciousness to an open, wise mind. Practice of some sort is necessary to open the mind. With practice, the mind is transformed. An open mind is not flooded by emotional reactions or restricted by trapped unconscious material. An open mind gives space for keen perception, emotional stability, creativity, logical thought, and insight from the spiritual domain.

Telling and listening to stories creates a focus of attention in a relaxed manner. This focus strengthens over time by listening to and telling stories. In this relaxed state, a human's consciousness enters a liminal space marked by interconnection with others.

Emotional stability results because an open mind is not reactive to emotions. A focus of attention gives stability to the mind, so that emotions can come and go across the mindscape, like clouds in the sky. Also, a space opens so that unconscious material can naturally emerge and float away. This space allows creative insight from the personal unconscious. Further, an open mind unveils the *buddhi,* a Sanskrit word meaning the wisdom faculty. The *buddhi* is the connection to the spiritual domain and allows insight.

Overtime storytelling can become a practice, such that the mind becomes increasingly spacious, and openness becomes a natural state. Wisdom ensues.

Why This Book: Storytelling, Wisdom, and Archetypes

In 2018, I was in Europe on a bicycle trip in Provence, France, and then I went to the U.K. for a conference on psychological health. I had been researching and writing about archetypes. Ever since I started exploring imagery in the late 1980s, I thought I'd publish a popular book and give lectures on some circuit. It seems hubris has been my life's companion. In 1985, I gave a workshop on imagery and learning for the Los Angeles schools, and I thought I'd be on my way. I also presented a workshop for the Arizona Association of School Secretaries on imagery and relaxation. I introduced the idea of imagery to the association's participants, and they said to me, "Is this like napping?" And I responded, "Yes, it is," since when one experiences vivid imagery, the parasympathetic nervous system is activated. The parasympathetic nervous system is the part of the autonomic nervous system that is restorative. The heart rate decreases, blood pressure lowers, and alpha brain waves emerge.

I continued the idea of being a workshop maven. In 1994, I created a workshop on imagery and physical healing for nurses in Paradise Valley, Arizona, focusing on psychoneuroimmunology. The topic was the use of imagery to change the physiological process for physical healing. The syllables mean "psycho," visualizing; "neuro," increasing neurotransmitters, such as endorphins; and "immunology," the increase in endorphins. For example, one can lock into immune cells and change their speed and direction. The concept was based on Candice Pert's research, which showed that the nervous system talks to the immune system. Before her research, the different systems of the body were thought to be independent—the nervous, cardiovascular, immune, and muscular systems. Pert showed that immune cells actually have receptors that neurotransmitters can lock into, a key that fits a lock.

As my research and writing progressed, I presented at conferences in Japan, Cuba, London, Mexico, and in many cities in the U.S. But I never became a work-shopper who "caught fire," nor did I receive a slew of invitations. I thought my archetype book would do the trick. When I started that book around 2012, I wanted to write something that would sell. That hubris gene was still active. But more than that, I thought I had developed some ideas that would help others. As a Zen practitioner who said the Bodhisattva vow each Sunday for many years—"The many beings are numberless; I vow to save them"—I thought I was developing a theory and, more importantly, a practice to open people's minds to the inner world for healing, learning, and insight. Of course, I had written many things, including a curriculum design book, an imagery book, books for youth (with my non-profit, the WHEEL Council), and many research articles. But I never got traction. I thought, "This book—yes, this book—is going to do the trick," as I was working on the draft of *Archetypal Imagery.*

I lived in Flagstaff, Arizona, 60 miles south of the Grand Canyon, and 30 miles north of Sedona, the New Age Mecca of pink jeeps going to vortices. In Sedona, there were also statues of javelinas, pig-like animals from the peccary family of South America, who roamed the prickly pears and junipers of central Arizona. Sedona is a hub for educated retirees, attorneys, investors, and potential mystery writers. I thought there must be a writer's group. I found one, and I was determined to be humble. I would submit my chapters for review and crack the nut of writing a book that sells.

We met every few weeks and submitted our work for the next week. A retired attorney wanted to write Jack Reacher-type novels. Another woman seemed to want to become Tolkien by writing fantasy chapters. We were led by a very together woman who worked as a professional editor. My writing was dissected and criticized. I took quite a bit of criticism, and then I would write and rewrite. But one night, the criticism seemed a bit vitriolic. I drove home on Highway 89, a gorgeous drive from Sedona to Flagstaff through Oak Creek Canyon, climbing 5,000 feet up to the Mogollon Rim to Flagstaff—one of the most beautiful drives in the world. I enjoyed driving and taking hairpin corners. My first husband liked Formula One racing, and he taught me to speed up in curves to take advantage of centrifugal force. I must admit, I was driving home a bit fast, finally breaking out of my false humility to be angry at the feedback that I thought was totally unfair.

I went home and looked up every member of the group on Amazon to see what they had published—nada. I was released from trying to learn how to write a popular book and resigned myself to the fact that I was an academic and had to be true to my ilk. I was pleased when I finally published *Archetypal Imagery*. Jessica Kingsley is a reputable publisher, but I was on my own in terms of marketing. One of my good friends in my Zen group, who was a successful writer, read the book. Her name is Annette McGivney, and she published a popular book, *The Pure Land*, a combination memoir and true crime about a Japanese tourist who was murdered in Havasupai in the Grand Canyon. I trusted her judgment. She got the significance of the book—the use of archetypal identification to open space in the mind to clear emotions and connect with the spirit within. This made me happy, and I was hopeful about the future. I got a lot of good reviews on my Amazon page, but for most people, the book seemed too abstract. People didn't quite get the topic, as archetypes are a bit esoteric, being an energy pattern in the collective unconscious.

However, this book advanced my journey to help me and others in how to connect with the natural forces of human development to open the inner world to wisdom. My path from yoga to imagery to storytelling pointed to the importance of the main character in stories being an archetype. Being inspired by Jungian psychology, particularly of what Jung called the Self, strengthened my interest in archetypes for the book. Archetypes are the conduit to the Self. I had thought at one time that Jung's Self was the same as the Hindu Vedantic *atman,* the spiritual self. However, there are some subtle differences. For Jung, the Self was the whole of the person. Sometimes I think of a mandala representing what Jung conceived of as the Self, and the *atman* is only a part of the mind connected to the energetic and spiritual domain. I am not sure that talking about these parts of the mind is helpful. The main point is that Jung posits that opening the unconscious mind allows awareness to be with the Self connected to the collective unconscious, and the Vedantic view is that there is a part of the mind called the *atman* connected to the spiritual or energetic domain. Both are about opening the deeper parts of the mind toward wholeness for greater potential, psychological maturity, and spiritual insight.

One of my favorite Jungian scholars is Edward Edinger. In his book, *Ego and Archetype,* he talks about the ego-Self axis. Most of us are unaware that we have a Self. We think we are the stream of thoughts in the mind generated by the ego. The ego is a psychodynamic structure that creates stability to integrate the array of sensations in the perceptual screen. Emotional maturity happens when the ego takes a supporting role in consciousness, as opposed to trying to control it, allowing conscious awareness to open to the Self. In Edinger's model, in the mature mind, consciousness can move fluidly and agilely between the ego and the Self. Over the years, I have been trying to formulate how to tap into a natural psychodynamic process that could help a person move into the consciousness of being aware of the Self, or the complete mind-body, and I have developed a wise mind-body model.

The Wise Mind-Body Model

In this model, the ego is no longer in control of consciousness, as noted by the dotted line. This allows consciousness to be open to emotional, physical, and spiritual dimensions. Human development prompts a transformed being in line with Trungpa's definition that a wise person has consciousness that is spacious, warm, and friendly. This requires clearing and opening the mind to the inner world.

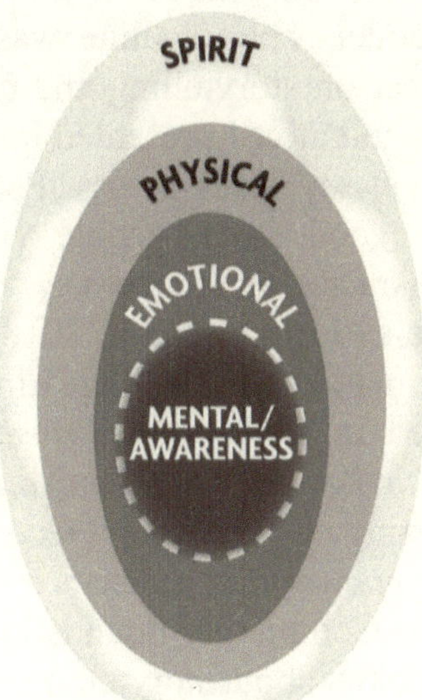

The Wise Mind-Body

Archetypal Imagery is my ode to using identification with an archetype to accomplish the transformation of consciousness. I saw it as a psychodynamic in that people naturally identify with archetypes even though they don't know it. If one can prompt this on a conscious level—*voila!*—there is movement toward wisdom. The book contains theoretical background on the topic and proposes some possible archetypes with quizzes and stories, including coaching sessions that could be used to prompt this. Included are stories of people who have used my method. But the book missed the mark. It was too esoteric or too abstract for people to relate to. I taught many graduate clinical psychology students using the book, and when we went through the sessions together, it worked. However, without individual coaching, the book did not seem to be effective at moving people toward wisdom as a standalone. I thought I needed another way to communicate what I knew about transforming the being to wisdom. And that leads me to writing this book, *Storytelling, Wisdom, and Archetypes.*

I was going to France for a bicycle trip and wanted to deduct my trip. I found a conference in London on Health Psychology that would work at the end of the trip. It seemed to fit my non-profit, the

WHEEL Council's work, using the curriculum from the *Storytelling for Empowerment* model. The deadline was approaching, and I pulled out an old paper on storytelling and massaged it. As I was working on the paper and after I presented it, I thought storytelling was the medium to get my ideas across. People like stories, and when listening to a good story, people visualize pictures frequently—the main character, an archetype.

The paper I presented in London in 2018 is titled "Indigenous Storytelling: Transformation for Healing, Emotions and Spirituality." It was published in *Conference Proceedings, International Scholarly and Scientific Research and Innovation.* I had written a lot about storytelling starting in 1992 when I received my first grant for the *Storytelling for Empowerment* substance abuse prevention program from the Arizona Community Foundation.

One was a little booklet about storytelling and prevention, which described the storytelling cycle and the purposes of story. Some of the most important points in that booklet were having respect for humans and nature; seeing the continuity of life from the past, present, and future; honoring culture and family identification; and providing maps of how to face and navigate adversity. I knew that humans had used storytelling for centuries to help people know where they came from and where they were going, giving metaphoric and psychological security about the existential questions of life.

In the article, I also reviewed the emotional components of story. The content of story is not only about heroes and heroines on adventures displaying courage, but also it is from the heart of the storyteller to the heart of the listener. Through the symbols and metaphors of story, listeners come in contact with unconscious material. Stories plant symbols and metaphors in people's hearts and minds, and these grow over time to provide resources for inner strength. By tapping the energy realm of the collective unconscious, stories can shift consciousness to inter-individual awareness. Stories open the inner world to wisdom.

It was a little bit of an odd conference in that it was not just about health psychology; the workshop organizers had advertised it for many other disciplines. So I was on a panel with someone from

Brazil who had researched counseling those with disabilities, and an engineer from Paris who researched evacuating the Metro during a crisis. This was a wild mix, but it was fun. One thing about research is that it is always invigorating to learn about new results. It seemed like grad students and professors from all over the world had come to London to get a notch on their curriculum vitae and enjoy a cosmopolitan city.

The days after the conference, I took the train to Brighton and found a hotel on the seaside. I realized that over the years, from beginning the *Storytelling for Empowerment* model in the early 1990s, I've been collecting stories from all over the world, including North America, Greenland, Scotland, Japan, China, the Yoruba tribe in Africa, and more.

I decided that writing a book about storytelling instead of archetypes might be more accessible for people to open the inner world to wisdom. Engaging with stories moves one's consciousness to the mythic realm, which clears and calms the mind. I decided to collect all my archived stories and work through them to find common themes.

In my role as a professor at Fielding Graduate University in Santa Barbara, California, I teach qualitative research. Qualitative research often collects interviews, stories, or narratives from a select group of participants who meet the criteria to answer a research question. The philosophy of this research method is that studying people in the context of their lives is a way to find out relevant information instead of isolating variables that can be measured.

Then the researcher interacts with the narratives in reading, rereading, bracketing possible bias, and eventually finding patterns that could be themes. Stories are a way of helping people find their inner characteristics to cope and to thrive.

The Stories in This Book

I spent time reviewing the stories I'd collected to find themes, which is what this book is about. The first step was to pull the stories I'd collected from my archive. These are the stories I've used.

Keep on Steppin' is an African American tale about a slave named Jim who saves the master's children and is promised his freedom. However, he has to work for several more years. The master is surprised when Jim actually takes the proffered freedom and walks away.

The Dragon's Robe is a Chinese tale about a weaver, Kwan Yin, whose perseverance rids the country of corrupt lords and helps the Emperor regain his throne. Kwan Yin is the Chinese name for the Tibetan Avalokiteśvara, the Buddha of compassion.

Juan Bobo is a Mexican folktale of how the innocence of a son on a quest to help his mother brings riches to the family. It shows the humor of taking advice literally and the benefits of a pure heart.

Ramayana is a complicated tale from the ancient Hindu text of the Vedas that showcases Rama, an incarnation of Vishnu, the preserver in the Hindu pantheon. Rama is noble and humble and defeats the ten-headed monster Ravana. Rama's betrothed Sita, his monkey god friend Hanuman, and his brother Lakshmana play important roles.

Xenophobe is my own story of dragons breaking the cycle of violence. Xenophobe is a young dragon who lives high above the tree line with his family in the mountains. His father, Ebony, is only a vague memory to Xenophobe, but he is happy with his mother and with his mate, Citron. He discovers that male dragons enact a fatal parody with humans to give the illusion of peace.

Coyote is my own story of a silly coyote rejecting help but persevering to help his pups. Owl, Eagle, Otter, and Bear play important parts, and Coyote's pups keep him present.

The Four Directions is a Hopi creation story about the peoples of the four directions developing their gifts. Then he/she, the creator, gives each of the peoples of the four directions a unique gift. On their migrations, they interact and share their gifts. But when jealousy erupts, a few of the peoples come forward to learn from each other in tolerance.

John the True is a Celtic tale about John's loyalty to his King and the tests that he navigates to save his King. This is another complex tale. It is about John's King falling in love with a painting of a beautiful Princess—with hair as black as ebony, cheeks as red as roses, and skin as white as ivory—who lives in an enemy kingdom. John uses trickery to capture her, and on the voyage home, Ravens give him messages of doom. He can prevent the doom at the risk of his own life. The story continues until the King's twin sons save John.

Buffalo Woman is an Osage tale about a man who falls in love with a beautiful woman who can morph into a buffalo. He must become a buffalo to reunite with his wife and daughter. He dies and is reborn as a buffalo.

Gaia is a Greek myth about Earth's mother goddess, who has to use trickery with her husband and son to protect life. Gaia and her mate, Ouranos, have many children, including the Cyclops, whom Ouranos decides to eat. Later, her son Cronos wants her to do away with his son Zeus, since there is a prophecy that Zeus will dethrone him. Gaia saves her offspring from the patriarchy.

Lilith is the story of Adam's first wife, who was thrown out of Eden for wanting to be on top during sex. She came back as the serpent to tempt Eve, bringing knowledge to the world. Lilith is a primeval being with claws for feet and wings to fly.

Isis, an Egyptian goddess representing the Nile, tricks the sun god Re into telling her his name and gains his power. Isis is one of a set of quintuplets. She marries her brother Osiris. Their brother Seth is jealous and kills Osiris. Isis and her sister Nephthys fly to find Osiris's body on a sand bar. She mates with him and births the great Pharaoh Horus.

Ganesha is the Hindu elephant god, the son of Shiva, and one of the triumvirate termed "the destroyer." Ganesha's mother, Parvati, asks him to guard her while she is bathing to stave off Shiva's amorous advances. Shiva is furious and takes off Ganesha's head. Parvati implores Shiva to replace her son's head, and the nearest one is that of an elephant. Ganesha becomes a deity who removes obstacles and bestows beneficence.

The Children is a Yoruba tale. Many African Americans in the U.S. trace their lineage to the Yoruba tribe of West Africa. In this story, a wise woman is consulted by the villagers for herbs to cure infertility. It is successful, and afterward, the people of the village come to help the elder with repairs and yard work, but soon they forget her. When their children become sick, they remember her again, and she again helps them with herbs. They never forget her again.

Deirdre is a Celtic tale of rivalry among kings and nobles. This is a very famous and complex tale. When Deirdre was born, her father was told that she would be the death of kings. So her father hides her away. She grows into a beautiful woman. One day, the king saw Deirdre and fell madly in love. In her innocence, she agrees to be betrothed. Life happens, and subsequently, a prince and his two brothers come into the woods. This time, Deirdre falls in love. She goes with the prince, and the king goes through machinations to kill the prince and his brothers. Deirdre throws herself into his grave.

Avalokiteśvara is about a Tibetan Buddhist deity who embodies compassion. He is a bodhisattva who has taken a vow not to go to nirvana until all sentient beings can join him. He is overcome with the enormity of human suffering, and his head breaks into many pieces. He is transported to the pure land with the Buddha, and he is given eleven heads and one thousand arms to relieve suffering.

Sophia and Claude is my own story of a multiracial woman from a time that seems like the future but also like the past. Sophia is a bookbinder's daughter and excels at binding books by hand. She wins a contest for "the most successful woman." Later, she learns that she has been tricked into sacrificing herself to a dragon, Claude, to keep him from terrorizing the village. Surprises await as she learns the dragon's earth wisdom.

The White Spider is a Paraguayan tale about love between a humble man and the chieftain's daughter. They are thwarted by class. Love conquers all when the man finds the gift of a beautiful lace shawl spun by his friend, the white spider.

The Shaman Story is an Inuit tale from Iceland about the many tests a young man goes through to become a shaman.

Cinderlad is an Italian story about a mysterious monster eating a poor man's crops every June 24th, St. John the Baptist Day. Cinderlad is the youngest brother of three who is ridiculed by his brothers, as he sits in the cinders of their hearth. Over time, Cinderlad, although humble and self-effacing, faces the monster and brings riches to the family.

Coyote and Cottontail: Cottontail Cheats Death is a story in a book from a Navajo education project. Coyote's frailty and audacious nature is apparent in the story, as he chases Cottontail to eat him, but Cottontail tricks Coyote in roasting his own behind.

Throughout this book, I'll return to each of these stories at different times to point out how storytelling and identification with the archetypes lead to wisdom. These stories shed light on the definition of wisdom, how the structures of story give a map for facing adversity and navigating life, and how the characters in stories are archetypes to open the unconscious in a safe manner for spiritual insight from the collective unconscious. The stories will also show the indigenous philosophy of aligning with nature for balance and harmony. Finally, examples from stories of themes such as acceptance, tests, bravery, beauty, and death/rebirth give readers a roadmap on their path to wisdom. Several of the stories I return to again and again since they have a multi-layered meaning. These are *The Children, The Dragon's Robe, John the True,* and *Cinderlad.*

Please know the repetition of these stories is by design. Rather than require you to flip back and forth to a story's summary to remember the main plot points, I repeat the salient storylines for you. And doesn't this imitate the way we take in stories as children? We want to hear them over and over again, and with each retelling, we may learn something different on our path toward wisdom.

Chapter One: The Journey

This book gleans virtues from world-sourced stories—and a few of my own imagination—to discover how humans can embody wisdom. The stories showcase five virtues to move humans toward wisdom. Stories are an ancient human technology for passing on culture, including values, beliefs, and attitudes. They also contain wisdom. Stories create maps for facing adversity, be it walking through fire, slaying a dragon, or finding helpers for transformation and metaphors for the ups and downs of daily life.

I've worked with stories for over twenty years to help young people thrive amid poverty and racism and to help adults find emotional health and spiritual awareness. Through doing this work, I've collected cultural stories from all over the world, created curricula with stories, became a storyteller, and learned the patterns and rhythms of a story. This allowed me to merge with the oral tradition and use these patterns to create stories. My archive of stories includes Celtic, European, African, North American, Indian, and South American cultures. Some are elaborate and complicated. Some are simple and compelling. But all contain patterns of human behavior that solve problems and create the wisdom to make people's lives work.

"Wisdom" is often defined as the combination of experience and knowledge. Wisdom also has the ineffable elixir that deepens both knowledge and experience. Possibly, this is insight or intuition since telling and listening to stories creates space for access to the deep wells of human experience in liminal spaces.

This book is about the wisdom that stories teach. Thomas Aquinas, as reported by author Kenneth Garcia, said that a synonym for wisdom is *lifeability.* This is what I mean when I say stories tell humans how to make their lives work. Saint Thomas Aquinas was born in Roccasecca, Italy, in 1224, and he died in a monastery near Terracina, Italy, in 1275. As a philosopher and theologian, he was an influential writer in medieval times. He had eight siblings, and his mother was a countess of lower nobility. At his birth, it was predicted that he would be a monk and a famous scholar. At five years old, he was sent to an abbey to train with Benedictine monks. As a child, he often asked the question, "What is God?"

Saint Thomas Aquinas received a classical education, studying Aristotle and attending the University of Naples. Afterward, he joined the Dominican monks, who were considered radical at that time. As a result, his family kidnapped him for deprogramming and sent him to Germany to study so that he could teach in Paris. As a freethinker, Thomas worked to reconcile theology and philosophy, which were in conflict at that time. He wrote about reason and free will, focusing on practical everyday life. Thomas had visions that informed his work and writing. Near his death, he went on a walking pilgrimage, but he was forced to stop at a monastery, where he died.

Saint Thomas Aquinas's definition of wisdom as lifeability possibly emerged from his mission to merge philosophy with reason. If people have lifeability, they can handle life's ups and downs, figure out how to solve problems, pull in resources, accept and release emotions, and build relationships. Lifeability includes inner strength and stability. There is a fulcrum that allows one to regain balance after the ups and downs of life. "To love and to work" is an ability that denotes a healthy human, a phrase often attributed to Freud, as reported by Alan Elms. Wisdom combines practicality, work, and emotional balance with knowledge and experience to create lifeability.

James Taylor wrote a song, "Secret of Life," for his 1977 album, *JT.* In the lyrics, he says, "The secret of life is enjoying the passage of time." He says we should enjoy the ride and show some style. A beautiful lyric is "the secret of love is opening up your heart."

Taylor's song adds another dimension to lifeability, emphasizing the experience of inner peace through accepting the flow of life. Wisdom is not just knowledge and experience but also a changed inner world that allows the mysterious elixir of deep knowing, accompanied by inner peace. The transformation of the inner world can be felt and touched, and it radiates from a person.

Wisdom is the goal of human development. People treasure those among them who are considered wise because they seemingly transcend the human condition. They make sound decisions, give astute advice, espouse sage words, balance emotions with clarity, perceive clearly, and anchor society toward charity to others. There is a theory that human consciousness is evolving toward goodness. In his 2012 book, *The Better Angels of Our Nature: Why Violence Has Declined,* Steven Pinker claims that humans have become less violent over time. Some may disagree with this, but Pinker offers a compelling argument that, over time, human civilization has progressed toward less violence, from feeding people to the lions to the establishment of the UN's International Court of Justice. Humans can find ways to move themselves and others to wisdom to continue this evolution.

Western psychologists map human development across many domains, including intellectual, emotional, spiritual, moral, and cognitive. Indigenous medicine men and women look to help their tribes and tribal members become balanced and whole. In both traditions, the hope is that humans can grow into their wise potential. This can happen by cultivating a calm, clear mind that opens to the creative force and the best of the human spirit. This requires a transformation of consciousness.

Consciousness is the inner topography of the mind that an individual experiences. For much of the time, people's inner experiences are chains of thoughts, almost like the crawler of breaking news posted at the bottom of the screen during news broadcasts. The mind is full of worries, plans, noises, memories, and repeating thoughts, along with sensations of anger, love, pleasure, fear, and nervousness. Humans work to quiet this barrage with methods such as religious practices, relationship work, psychological growth, love for others, and even love for oneself. This transformation of consciousness creates space for the mind to touch inner wisdom.

According to Ram Dass in his 1974 book, there are multiple ways of transforming consciousness. Even though he first started with LSD, he looked at other methods to find a way that would sustain such expanded states. He noted *pranayama*, yogic breath practices, and right action. I propose that telling and hearing stories can also contribute to such a transformation of consciousness.

In this book, I interlace my personal experiences that I believe transformed my consciousness to inner calm and clarity with my studies as a psychologist and the areas of yoga, imagery, emotional healing, and storytelling. I do not purport to have a constant state of calm and clarity. I'm not a yogi in a cave in the Himalayas, sitting in an emotionless state. But I consciously have access to such a state that I can touch, sometimes in an uninvited manner and sometimes by choice. After forty-some years of being a psychologist working to discover the means for the transformation of consciousness, I think I've found some things. It all started with a vision while doing yoga. But you will see how it grows into storytelling through this book.

Much of my storytelling knowledge comes from Joseph Campbell's work on myth. I prefer to use the word "story." As Paula Gunn Allen notes, when non-indigenous scholars use the word "myth," they insinuate that the content is false or inaccurate. But according to Allen, myth articulates wisdom that is not expressed in other forms.

My Journey

> "Myth is the secret opening through which the inexhaustible energies of the cosmos pour into the human cultural manifestation."
> -Joseph Campbell

To set the stage for the book and how I grew into the vehicle of storytelling for wisdom, I present a bird's-eye view of my journey. As the book progresses, I'll fill in detail about my career that led me to this point.

I was always captivated by how humans came to know about their world. Coming of age during the 1970s, I caught the human potential fever. As a psychology graduate student, I wanted to empower children by tapping into their natural learning tendencies. I was a consultant to inner-city and rural schools throughout the U.S.

I sat in classrooms and watched extremely bright students struggle to do what was asked of them. I knew there was a better way. Simultaneously, I was caught up in the Eastern spiritual practices of yoga, which promised enlightenment and altered states of consciousness. With obvious hubris, my friends and I joked that we could be enlightened in our lifetime and stop the cycle of reincarnation.

Over time, these seemingly disparate threads of enhancing learning and of experiencing altered states of consciousness intertwined to lead me on a journey. I saw enhanced learning and spiritual transformation on a continuum to becoming a whole person. I wanted that for myself, and I wanted to help others to do the same. I found the definition of this transformation as wisdom in Chögyam Trungpa's book *The Heart of the Buddha*. Wise people have compassion, friendliness, warmth, and a spacious mind. This was consistent with my view of wisdom. My quest became how to transform my consciousness into wisdom and how to help others do the same.

My journey has taken me betwixt and between liminal states to determine that storytelling is a natural human method for changing the topography of the inner world towards spaciousness. It's a space that prompts spiritual awareness and emotional strength to become wise. Spiritual awareness comes from a relaxed mind, where insights can move into awareness. The emotional strength comes from unconscious material unwinding. Both of these come from the liminal space created in the mind when telling and listening to story. The elements of my journey to storytelling show how I got there and how storytelling incorporates the elements to become wise.

Yoga: Focus the Mind

Through yoga practice, I experienced a focus on the mind and expansive visionary states, with a sense of interconnection with other life. I learned that the relaxed focus of attention was important and was the key to developing wisdom. Yoga did this. The relaxed focus of the mind allowed mind stuff—the Sanskrit word for this is *chitta*—to unwind and move out as it dissipated. This mind becomes more open and relaxed. During my years as a yogi, I learned that practicing a relaxed focus of attention could transform the inner world and create a liminal state for spiritual insights. I also learned that, instead of trying to control emotions, to be "spiritual," the best route was to be humble with emotions, accepting them and letting them come and go as clouds in the sky. Yoga was a key in my journey towards wisdom, and I also discovered that something more was needed to heal and release emotions. That will become clearer when the path leads to imagery. When I heard people in the spiritual community talking about controlling emotions or not feeling, I was concerned.

During my undergraduate college years, 1966 through 1970, cataclysmic changes happened in my personal life and the societal subculture I inhabited. I loved college. During my freshman year at the University of Michigan, I literally lived at the library, with its vaulted ceiling and iconic green desk lamps. I even took naps in the library, waking up with bleary eyes and drool on my lips, but ready to tackle the next book. I loved the University of Michigan. I remember one night in the dorm following a fire drill, I got back to our room before anyone else and went straight back to studying. My roommates made fun of me because I was studying before anyone got back from the fire drill.

After doing yoga, I quieted my wild mind. I've always had a wild mind, as it was all over the place. I remember a time during graduate school at the University of Kansas when I was writing a paper about learning while I worked in a preschool for children with special needs. I spent a lot of time in the university library. At that time, there were no computers, but there were drawers and drawers of files with small cards. I loved those cards. They had a nice color, wheat or quinoa, which over time has become my favorite color. Plus, the font on the cards was often weirdly smudged with indecipherable pencil marks, which was somehow endearing. I spent many hours in libraries sorting through those little cards to find the right book. Sometimes my mind would race so fast that I thought I was going to explode. I'd get an idea, then it would connect to another idea, and at a certain point, I'd have to get out of the library and run around. (Most people think of Kansas as flat, but not Lawrence, Kansas. I can attest to that, as I rode my Motobecane ten-speed up and down

Mount Oread to get from the preschool to the library.) As I searched the card file, my mind raced with all the ideas I was processing to make the curriculum work for kids who learned differently. The ideas came faster and faster, and I needed help. Yoga was my answer.

I could use those library cards, find books, take notes, and work for hours. I knew yoga had remarkable effects on the mind. What followed was many years and many ways of documenting a mechanism that moved one to a transformation of consciousness.

Graduate school, from 1970 to 1978, was an exciting time for me. I loved working with children and collecting data. As a product of the baby boomer generation, I felt that (borrowing a phrase used by my mother) the Earth was my oyster. I continued yoga practice and reading. Ram Dass had two books, *Be Here Now* and *The Only Dance There Is*, which I loved. I was drawn to Ram Dass for a number of reasons. One was that he had been a child psychologist, and I was getting a degree in developmental and child psychology. I liked that he had a solid grounding in both psychoanalysis and developmental psychology. Second, after my visionary experience during yoga, I was interested in Eastern spiritual practice. After realizing LSD was a dead end, since one came back down again, Ram Dass went to India and practiced *pranayama* to find a sustained transformation of consciousness. His quest was exemplified in this quote: "Do I feel I've achieved the state of mind before with LSD…? Under these conditions I have gone into states that are comparable to almost all of the states I have experienced with LSD, not all of them but almost all of them. I see that it is a method very similar in certain ways, in that it forces, it overrides, certain habits of thought and places."

Vedantic Philosophy

People think *pranayama* is a group of breathing exercises. Actually, *pranayama* is much bigger than breathing exercises. According to Swami Vivekananda, *prana* is the life force, and as one practices *pranayama*, one learns to work in the energy field of creation. In yoga, there are eight limbs: *yamas* (ethical rules), *niyamas* (health practices), *asana* (physical poses), *pranayama* (breath control), *pratyahara* (withdrawal of senses), *dharna* (concentration), and *samadhi* (union). I had stumbled across the practice of yoga while watching Lilias Folan on PBS after a tiring and stressful day working in a preschool and teaching undergraduates.

Practicing yoga during graduate school had a profound effect on me. I thought it was the answer to help humans on their quest for wisdom. I had a vision during a yoga *asana,* or corpse pose. I saw the colors of the rainbow starting at my base chakra and going up through my chakras out the top of my head. I pursued yoga to relieve the stress of work and studying as a graduate student while also teaching preschool and undergraduate social science research. Yoga had an immediate effect on me. My mind was quiet. As a result, I delved into yoga philosophy and the Vedantic view of the mind, documented in the *Rig Veda*, an ancient Sanskrit text from around 1500 B.C. This philosophy posits the existence of a part of the mind called the *atman,* or the spiritual Self. The practice of yoga develops another part of the mind, the *buddhi, or* wisdom faculty, which allows the mind to connect with the *atman.* Making space by developing the *buddhi* gives the *atman* permission to present insight.

In Vedantic thought, there is an energy field from which material reality emerges. I knew this view was outside the paradigm of Western psychology. However, the Heisenberg uncertainty principle in physics might suggest that there is an energy domain. This principle is that a particle can be measured as momentum or position. It is uncertain whether matter is movement or a point in time. Also, due to my experiences with visions that seemed like non-ordinary reality, I thought developing a wisdom faculty to contact an energy field made sense.

I was interested in tapping into what I learned in yoga philosophy to unleash human potential. I realized in my quest to pursue enlightenment that I had much hubris. My awareness of being arrogant in considering the possibility of becoming enlightened was reinforced by other aspects of the human potential movement at the time. It was the beginning of the prosperity consciousness movement, too. My friends read Shakti Gawain's book *Creative Visualization* and somehow enlightenment became the same as getting wants and riches.

My Christian upbringing kicked in at this point in my journey. I thought that surely material rewards were not the aim of becoming enlightened. After all, Jesus said that you give with one hand when the other hand does not know about it. I also found support that prosperity was not the best path for transformation. In B.K.S Iyengar's book *Light on Yoga,* he said that *siddhis* come on the spiritual path. *Siddhis* are gifts—heightened intuition, for example. Iyengar said that even though gifts come, it's best for a person to not pay attention to them. It was important to keep one's eye on the prize: enhanced awareness, not material gain.

During this era of my life and work, I defined what I considered the goal of human development as wisdom, not scaling the heights toward enlightenment. I presented a paper at the Transpersonal Psychology Conference and published a book entitled *How to Focus the Distractible Child*, focusing on yoga and the idea of using self-talk to focus attention.

As a baccalaureate student, I learned that I could graduate with honors by completing a project and enrolling in a seminar. This led me to find a preschool on campus for exceptional children in the Department of Human Development and Family Life (HDFL). I was a bit stressed during this time. I'd bike to the HDFL preschool, mix tempera paints, sing preschool songs, run some research studies, and teach statistics for undergraduates in the afternoon. I was also doing dissertation research, working with Project Follow-Through, a kindergarten through third-grade program that my PhD advisor ran in Indianapolis. I went there once a month to train teachers in his educational model.

The stress of this business led me to yoga. I took a deep dive into Hindu philosophy when yoga helped relieve my stress. This was in the mid-1970s, when The Beatles were learning transcendental meditation with Maharishi Mahesh Yogi, and when Ram Dass had gone to India to study with Maharaj Ji. He realized that LSD-expanded consciousness wasn't the end-all. After one went up, one would come down. He wanted a sustainable transformation of consciousness. That was why he went to India. Ram Dass, along with The Beatles, was a symbol of cultural change that opened young people to yoga and meditation.

Ram Dass learned *pranayama* breathing exercises in an ashram in India, where he had gone to re-create the changes in consciousness that LSD had done, but without the LSD and in a more sustainable way. Ram Dass experienced and was interested in changes of consciousness. I also became entranced by expanded consciousness after the twelve-hour T-group and by my spontaneous imagery vision while doing yoga. As part of the cultural milieu of the 1970s, interest in expanded consciousness was at its peak. Psychologists like Ram Dass and others like Abraham Maslow, who studied peak experiences as documented in his 2013 book *Toward a Psychology of Being*, wanted to discover ways to unlock human potential by using more of the mind's capacity.

Those who have experienced changes of consciousness judge them as undeniable. Some call this expanded consciousness, and this state can be accompanied by feelings of bliss and interconnectedness with nature and other life. Ram Dass first experienced this with LSD and then later through his *pranayama* practice. I had a taste of it during the early recollection exercise and then during *savasana*. I made it my mission to explore and to teach others the ways of changing consciousness, which eventually led to hearing and listening to stories. Ram Dass said that there were multiple ways of changing consciousness, and amazingly, I found that the ancient tradition of storytelling was one way of helping people enter a liminal state, the threshold to expanded consciousness.

Iyengar Yoga

My visionary experience during *savasana* was possibly like Ram Dass' LSD experiences, but mine were through only yoga *asana*. I liked that Ram Dass learned that the "highs" were not the end, but the goal of spiritual practice was the transformation of consciousness. Yoga became a way of life for me. In addition to subscribing to *Yoga Journal*, I traveled to workshops in San Francisco to study a yoga system taught by B.K.S. Iyengar.

I became an avid yogi after my early transcendent experience. I loved Iyengar yoga, and I found it through the advice of Judith Lasater, a columnist for *Yoga Journal*. By then, I had two young children, and I wanted to take my practice further. I wrote to her, and she told me about the Yoga Institute of San Francisco. I visited there several times, and I was also blessed to go to a conference to see Iyengar. It was amazing, as there were yogis from all over the world and from the yoga practice all over San Francisco.

One night at the main hotel, Iyengar spoke, and I felt I received *darshan*, or a religious sight of a deity that changed consciousness. As he spoke, Iyengar's energy became this huge white energy of a lion moving throughout the entire hotel conference hall. Iyengar yoga had a reputation for being hardcore. We Iyengar practitioners would say, "Give us a hard pose." Although it was intense, the gift of Iyengar was alignment and awareness, and even though the poses were extended, we were admonished to bring our attention within and keep a focus to allow our bodies to release. It was such a wonderful conference.

As a psychologist, I was interested in what was happening in the mind to allow the expanded consciousness that could lead to *samadhi*. From my training, I knew that repressed emotions would eventually erupt, and when the ego was identified with "being spiritual," it could get in the way of opening the mind to awareness. Over time, I realized that many people who did yoga were really denying their emotional lives. Yoga was effective in calming the mind, but more was needed for emotional health and strength. I realized it wasn't just "being spiritual" but emotional awareness and health needed to be part of the path.

Expanded states of consciousness are often accompanied by visions or thinking in images. Yoga and Buddhism teach that quieting the mind and stopping its chatter allow one to come into contact with the deep part of the mind connected to spirit. Emptying the mind, quieting the mind, and opening the mind is the path. I thought imagery as a natural human cognitive ability was a way to wisdom, a way to sense the "whatness" of reality.

In the Vedantic model, there are five divisions of the mind: the *manas*, the sensory thoughts; the *chitta*, the memory bank; the *ahankar*, the sense of "I-ness"; the *buddhi*, the wisdom faculty; and the *atman*, the spirit self. The purpose of yoga practice, not just *asana* (physical poses) but the whole system of yoga, is to quiet the *manas*, *chitta*, and *ahankar* to develop the *buddhi* as a vehicle to open to the *atman*. This allows awareness to sense the spirit within and the interconnection to others. The yoga system allows the transformation of consciousness, focusing attention inside the body in a relaxed, almost passive way. It is the way that one can create alpha brain waves, a relaxed, restorative state. I saw that thinking in images would do the same thing. I was on a quest to help people create an open awareness so that they could connect with their inner spirits and wisdom. I thought that maybe imagery could do the same thing as the practice of yoga.

I integrated my yoga practice with my psychology training. I particularly liked learning from Carl Rogers, one of the founders of humanistic psychology. He posited that there is a creative force in the unconscious. The idea is that opening the mind to contact the creative force leads a person to healing and growth and even to self-actualization. This sounded a lot like the *atman* from the Vedanta model. Rogers taught how to navigate uncomfortable emotions. One needed a safe place for expression, and then one could feel emotions and accept them. The creative force would act to integrate emotions, defusing their charge and prompting awareness.

Yoga and Oregon

My family had moved to Coos Bay, Oregon, to be by the ocean after living in the wheat fields of Kansas for a long time. After graduate school, I got into adult learning in 1980, when many colleges were shutting down as liberal arts schools and reopening as institutions focused on adult learners to match the demographics of those seeking BA degrees. Since I knew a lot about learning theory, it was a fit for me to work for programs capitalizing on self-direction for adults. These programs benefit from adult experiences, allowing personal values to be infused in college programs.

I worked for Marylhurst Education Center in the Portland area, which had an extension program in Coos Bay. Even though I was well-suited to create BA programs for working adults, my heart stayed with the idea of working with children. Because of this, I started a yoga class for children. Since yoga had helped me focus, I knew it could help younger people focus. I received a PhD in developmental and child psychology in 1978 and wanted to blend my experiential and intellectual knowledge to help children.

In Coos Bay, I found yoga friends. One was a member of Yogi Bhajan's 3HO—Healthy, Happy, Holy Organization—an organization documented by Doris Jakobsh, which was designed to bring Sikh Dharma to the West. "Dharma" means "teaching," and "Sikhism" is a monotheistic religion founded in the fifteenth century in Punjab, India, that rejected the caste system. Bhajan brought 3HO to the West, and people have probably seen adherents, who are noticeable by their white turbans.

Sikhism is a large religion, and Yogi Bhajan created a subset of it and brought it to the U.S. At one time, they had restaurants, and I ate at them in Tempe, Arizona, in Amsterdam, and the Netherlands. They still produce and sell Yogi Tea with great little sayings on the packaging. While living in Coos Bay, I attended my Sikh friend's yoga class. We did the breath of fire, and she exhorted us to relax our abdomens. I attended yoga classes with another friend at the library. We even got written up in the local newspaper. When my family and I moved to Prescott, Arizona, I did yoga in my daughter's second-grade classroom, still convinced that yoga could help children focus their attention.

During that time, Ritalin was the treatment of choice for learning-disabled children who were also diagnosed as hyperactive. I was not necessarily against Ritalin; as an eclectic educator and a psychologist, I advocated Western medicine as well as Eastern spiritual practices. Since yoga had such an effect on my ability to focus, I knew I was onto something. I was a big proponent of it. I think I annoyed people with my advocacy, particularly my family. I gave books on yoga for children to all my nieces and nephews. My sister-in-law said, "Right, we all need to be calm." She was making fun of me, but I wanted to say, "You're 100 percent right."

Based on my yoga class for children in Coos Bay, and my work with my daughter's second-grade class, I thought I was ready to bring yoga into the academic community to help learning-disabled children focus. My PhD program was in behavioral psychology, and sometimes this discipline gets a bad rap as being reductionist, meaning it reduces psychology to look only at behavior and external stimuli, either before or after behaviors., It is a solid criticism, but I think behaviorism has its place in understanding some things as long as it is not a complete worldview. One thing I liked about this approach was that it rejected labeling. The idea was that if one spent time diagnosing a person, the diagnosis might be the end, and not much was done to actually help the person.

I wrote a book on doing yoga with distractible children, *How to Focus the Distractible Child*. My book was more than yoga; it was how to teach a focus of attention. One area of research I included in the book related to yoga is self-talk. Distractible children seem to have difficulty with selective attention, or the ability to screen incoming stimuli. There is some debate over whether distractible children are initially overwhelmed by incoming stimuli or actually seek them out. In any case, self-talk functions to focus attention on what is in front of them. It is a natural human cognitive skill. For example, two-year-olds can be heard saying "no" aloud when trying to touch an electrical outlet. They have internalized what a parent has said to them.

Self-talk has similarities to yoga. In yoga, one takes one's attention inside to a certain area in the body, for example, the right arch of a foot in *virabhadrasana,* the warrior pose. One could call it a passive focus of attention. I also reviewed the cognitive process of imagery. Seeing pictures in the mind's eye also focuses attention. These techniques, along with yoga, could help a distractible child focus and teach attentional skills to be used in the future. All three of these techniques—yoga, self-talk, and imagery—evoke alpha brain waves accompanied by alert awareness.

I did a short application exercise, documented in the book, to apply my ideas. A third-grade teacher selected two students who had great difficulty working on their own during an independent reading period. The teacher gave individualized assignments and then circulated to check on the children. I took ten-second-interval observational data to record on-task attention for the two students during this individualized reading period. One student was on task 35 percent of the time, and the other one was on task 48 percent of the time. Then, for three weeks, I went to do yoga with the whole class for twenty minutes before the individualized reading period. In observation after the three weeks, those two students' on-task percentages increased to 69 percent and 74 percent. Of course, this was not a controlled study, and there are many possible confounds, as I was doing the training and the observation. I didn't have reliability on my observations, and there were only two students. But I was pleased with this exercise, and in a small way, it supported my idea of the importance of yoga in focusing the distractible child.

Yoga and Emotions

This was an important step on my path to explore ways to use humans' natural capacity to move to wisdom. I had hints from my own experiences with yoga of calming the mind to open to inner awareness. This was a step toward changing inner topography to a spacious mind. My subgroup included other people who were vegetarians and yogis, and we talked about enlightenment. Hindu thought was woven into the hippie mindset at that time, which envisioned enlightenment. One could transcend the human condition to experience *samadhi*, the last of the eight limbs of yoga —union with God, enlightenment. My friends and I had the hubris in thinking we could achieve *samadhi* in our lifetimes and stop the cycle of reincarnation. Even though Iyengar had taught that, instead of doing yoga to achieve, yoga was a process in itself for creating awareness. During my sojourn with yogis, I was also struck by people in the yoga community who were seemingly in denial about the emotions they were feeling. From my perspective, people thought that if they were spiritual—for example, doing yoga—they didn't need to feel anything. They could transcend emotions. Over time, I realized that many people doing yoga were really denying their emotional life. They assumed that "being spiritual" with the practice of yoga could make them impervious to the sometimes-chaotic emotional life within. It seemed that some yogis needn't worry about emotions, because they were spiritual. But what I observed was that some used their identity as yogi to actually be in denial of their emotional health.

I was very sensitive as a child, and as such, I'm sensitive as an adult when people aren't in touch with their emotions. I was the one who expressed my whole family's emotions. It was okay in my family to be cheerful or have repressed anger. But one couldn't really be angry, joyful, calm, or authentic. I was the one who expressed the family's feelings. This did not go over well, but maybe it is how I ended up as a psychologist.

I surmised that something else was needed besides yoga. From my training, I knew that repressed emotions would eventually erupt, and when the ego was identified with "being spiritual," it could get in the way of opening the mind to awareness. Over time, I realized that many people doing yoga were really denying their emotional life. Yoga was effective in calming the mind, but more was needed for emotional health and strength. Also, there was some backlash about yoga since some considered a weird Indian religion. I decided to shift my focus from yoga to imagery.

Imagery: Focusing the Mind and Transforming Emotions

Imagery practice taught an internal focus of attention that created space in the mind. In addition, I learned that visualizing emotions in the body could heal and transform those emotions to create emotional strength. With my study of imagery, I learned that focusing the mind on imagery or visualization could have the same benefits as yoga in creating a spacious mind that could help people become wise. Possibly stemming from the vivid images I had during yoga, I was drawn to the study of mental imagery in psychology. As a psychologist, I took a deep dive into studying the cognitive process of imagery, or thinking in internal sensations, particularly visual sensations.

Brain Research

The cognitive process of imagery is thinking in internal sensations of sight, sound, movement, taste, touch, and even smell. I was interested in the continuum of human development for potential and found research that imagery was very effective across a range of outcomes, besides the visions I had during yoga. Further, imagery had many other benefits. It could relax the body in terms of lowering heart rate or blood pressure. Imagery could even boost T cells' ability to fight the disease. For example, imagery could help physical healing by increasing immune cells, boosting creativity and memory, transforming difficult emotions, and mitigating trauma. Plus, it had additional effects like opening long-term memories and expanding perception.

Brain research was emerging when I was studying imagery. The advent of the PET scan showed that different parts of the brain did different things and spawned models like the right brain–left brain. I discovered work by brain physiologists that prompted me to focus on the limbic system, a rim-like structure threading underneath the cerebral cortex. The area of the brain that mediates imagery is called the amygdala. This structure in the center of the brain integrates sensory information and emotions and opens the memory banks. As a result, thinking in pictures, or using imagery, has powerful effects: relaxing the body, integrating emotions, and opening memory banks.

The cerebral cortex comprises the front lobes of the brain, identified with human brain activity. Most people think this is the most important part of the brain. However, I found the limbic system important as well. This structure in the brain organizes sensations, activates emotions, and includes autonomic nervous system activity. Because of the physiology of the limbic system, thinking in images has a direct line to activating its functions, particularly emotions. Imagery can help a person sense and transform emotions, which clears the mind. Using imagery to heal emotions, I judged, could move people to deeper transformative experiences.

Alfred Adler and Early Memories

Actually, imagery had been a thread in my life before I started doing yoga. Back in my undergraduate days, I worked at a mental health clinic in Oklahoma City while attending Bethany Nazarene

College. The clinic was led by a therapist who aligned with Alfred Adler's individual psychology.

Alfred Adler, as documented in Heinz Ansbacher's essay, was an Austrian psychologist, medical doctor, and psychotherapist who lived from 1870 to 1937. He created the theoretical school of Individual Psychology. To me, the most powerful concept from his take on psychology was the importance of early recollections. These were memories so vivid that a person could almost relive them as a movie playing on the mind's screen. These memories were often in pictures in the mind or an image.

During my first years of college, I studied math, transferred colleges three times, experienced the death of my boyfriend, acquired mentors, and found my calling at an Adlerian family clinic in the heart of an evangelical Christian city, Oklahoma City, Oklahoma. I loved working with children in the mental health clinic in Oklahoma.

It's a long story of how I got to Bethany Nazarene College. From the University of Michigan, I went to the University of Kansas with my boyfriend. I was a math major, and he was focused on English literature. During the ninth week of class, we were both at the university gym; I was swimming, and he was in a karate class. All of a sudden, someone ran into the swimming pool area and called me. My boyfriend was unconscious. When I came out of the dressing room after changing from my swimsuit, someone came up to me and said, "Your boyfriend has been taken to the hospital." It turned out that my boyfriend was at a karate class and had fallen. They had taken him to the university student medical center. Someone said, "Come with me," and I jumped on the back of a motorcycle. He took me to the student medical facility, but my boyfriend was not there. The motorcycle driver then took me to the city hospital.

When I walked into the emergency department, I actually saw my boyfriend on a gurney through a glass window. They were doing defibrillation on his heart, but it didn't work. In retrospect, I'm not sure I actually saw this. Would a hospital let a girlfriend see this? The attempt to resuscitate him didn't work. Paul died. He was 20, and I was 19, and I roiled in grief. After this happened, I spent days sleeping. I slept and slept because I would dream about him.

Paul was an Evangelical Christian. In part due to my grief, I transferred to Bethany Nazarene College in Oklahoma City. I went from the University of Michigan to the University of Kansas, and then to Bethany. I had been raised religious. My mom was the daughter of a Presbyterian minister, and she was very religious, carrying on his church-going tradition. Our family expectations and behavior were to go to Sunday school and Sunday worship service every week. My mom, Elizabeth, would get up early in the morning and start the roast that we would have for dinner after going to church.

I was good with music, so, in addition to this, the expectation was that I would sing in the choir, which I actually liked. I liked marching in before the service singing in my robe. My family's expectations were for me to go to church, go to school, achieve, and go to more school. As a kindergartener, I think I knew I was going to go to graduate school. I think this might be unique. I would like to find other people in the U.S. who thought at age five that they would go to graduate school. It seems that it would be a small sample. Sunday wasn't enough church in my family subculture. When I was a pre-teen, I went to youth fellowship every Sunday night, and I attended church camps in the summer. I remember they had us sign a pledge that we wouldn't drink alcohol. Later, when I was a freshman at the University of Michigan and going to sorority-fraternity parties, I would tell people I didn't drink. It must have been that Methodist training.

When my boyfriend and I were both at the University of Kansas, we were in love and going to make a life together. I was so happy, even though I was living in a dorm, but that was the *de rigueur* at the time. Women who were sophomores in college in 1967 lived in the dorms. I was there with a very dear friend from high school in Kansas City, Missouri. She had gone to the University of Missouri for her freshman year, and I had gone to the University of Michigan, but we were both back at the University of Kansas, living in the dorm together as roommates. We were swimmers, and she had been at the university pool swimming with me the evening that my boyfriend died.

After Paul died, I was lost. I stayed at KU, Rock Chalk Jayhawk, where we waved the wheat at football games, until that winter, when I transferred to Bethany Nazarene College. After he died, I was drawn to spend time with his family, and one of Paul's sisters lived in Oklahoma City. I went there for Thanksgiving after Paul had died in early fall. We attended a hockey game, and one of my friends from high school was there. She was attending Bethany Nazarene College. Somehow in my grief, it seemed to make sense for me to transfer there. I had decided to adopt Paul's religion. I prayed with him once and had an opening in my heart. But once I got there, I was still lost.

At Bethany Nazarene College, I liked the emotionality of the services—people yelling and crying and rejoicing—and I liked singing, which reminded me of my time in church choirs. But I was a fish out of water. I saw a lot of racism. My Christian upbringing was about civil rights. My parents participated in an anti-racism effort called Dinners for Ten. They were constructed of five couples, three Black and two White. They would meet monthly for dinner, rotating homes. My mother taught at Central High School in the inner city of Kansas City, Missouri. When I got to the Nazarene College in Oklahoma City in 1968, I noticed that there were White Nazarene churches and Black churches. I worked for the student newspaper, and I interviewed the pastor of the Black Nazarene church and wrote editorials such as "What color is God's skin?" I also organized a tutoring service for the urban area of Oklahoma City.

I was reeling with existential questions and traumas: "Why am I here? What am I going to do with my life?" There was a wonderful psychologist at the college, Dr. Forest Ladd, and I went to him with my problems. He gave me the Minnesota Multiphasic Personality Inventory (MMPI), a well-validated psychological test even used in courts to diagnose people. I was a little lost and a little out of my element. My experiences from my Methodist church taught me that miracles in the Bible were metaphors and that Christianity was stopping the racist redlining in Kansas City's real estate market. Being in an environment where witnessing to others was new and different, I thought I'd be a nurse, abandoning my goal of being a math major.

Although when I had taken biochemistry, I fainted when I took my own blood, so being a nurse wasn't a logical decision.

Dr. Ladd set me up at a community mental health clinic. I was assigned to work with a young boy who had enuresis, or bed-wetting. I played catch with him and did role plays with puppets. I'm not sure I helped, and also, in retrospect, I'm not sure it was appropriate for me to be working with a child at the age of twenty. But I was very grateful to have someone provide a setting that made sense to me. This was around 1968, and there was a phenomenon in counseling called T-groups (sensitivity-training groups). It was based on Carl Rogers's humanistic psychology theory of tapping the creative force in the unconscious in an emotionally safe environment. It also influenced Fritz Perls, also a humanistic psychologist, but his methods were more confrontational. At the Adlerian clinic, the psychologist led all the student interns in twelve-hour T-groups. It was transformative. Luckily, we were led by a competent psychologist who didn't let bullying take place when we confronted each other, which was a common occurrence.

During our T-group experience, the psychologist defined early recollections and led us on exercises to discover our very own early recollections. He said that these memories were significant because they were times when people made unconscious decisions about who they were in life. Early recollections are vivid memories from childhood. When he led us in an imagery exercise, I recalled a time very early in my life. I think I was about three, and I was golden and shiny in the image with a short white dress. I was in my backyard. We had a huge backyard, very green with an enormous lilac bush and irises. I was at the end of the yard, and my mother was standing far from me near the house. I felt so happy to be alive and full of golden light. I ran to my mother with my arms out, and she turned away and looked at something else. It wasn't really rejection, but it was inattention. It seemed like my decision about myself at that time was, "There is something wrong with me because my mother turned away."

Two things happened to me at Bethany Nazarene College in Oklahoma City, Oklahoma: I found love for working with children, and

I experienced the importance of imagery, or thinking in pictures, as in Adler's early recollection.

According to Adler, people's earliest memories are the most trustworthy approaches to their exploration of self. He termed these early recollections "the story of my life." These are not necessarily accurate memories, as they can be selections, distortions, or inventions that match people's fundamental view of their lives. Further, people can trace an action line from the earliest recollection to their inner world and the prototype of the style of life. For example, a depressed person might have the storyline "all my life I was unfortunate." Even though this may not have been accurate, it is an underlying theme that motivates actions and skews perception.

If people can evoke these early recollections and bring their memories to conscious awareness, then the storylines their memories represent can be examined and re-versioned for a more accurate, healthier story. To do this, the early recollections need to be invoked as vivid memories in an imagistic mode, such as in a dream. This was my first experience of the power of imagery, which became a very large part of my work. After my exploration at Bethany Nazarene College, I went back to the University of Kansas, not only as a math major but also with psychology in that mix.

The profound effect of imagery from the experience of early recollections in the Adlerian T-group came back to me in my search for a way besides yoga to transform consciousness. These early recollections contained my unconscious decision about who I was. Jeanne Achterberg, a groundbreaking psychologist in the field of imagery, had a profound effect on me as well. I saw her at an imagery conference in New York, and I was blown away by her presence, confidence, clarity, and breakthrough work on imagery. She had worked with O. Simonton at Southwestern Medical School in Dallas, who was using imagery to change levels of cancer cells.

Jeanne Achterberg and Imagery

Achterberg's 2002 book *Imagery and Healing: Shamanism and Modern Medicine* taught about the autonomic nervous system, which consists of two parts: the parasympathetic and the sympathetic. The parasympathetic is restorative, and the sympathetic acts to arouse. Imagery activates the parasympathetic system, which relaxes and restores the mind. I used her work to help people relax and open their awareness of emotional issues. I found with my students, and for myself, that thinking in pictures has an almost magical effect on the mind. I learned a lot about how to do imagery, which helped me later as I became a storyteller. Good storytelling creates pictures in the mind, and can have the same restorative functions as imagery.

In *Living the Wheel*, I write about how imagery can move the mind into the body. This gives a solid basis for intuitive work, since the body holds the mysteries of creation. Imagery accesses an underlying matrix of information in the unconscious mind which can explain the insight or "aha" phenomenon that accompanies the creative process. Jeanne Achterberg writes, "The thought process that invokes the senses: vision, audition, smell, taste, the sense of movement, position, and touch. It is the communication mechanism between perception, emotion, and bodily change. A major cause of both health and sickness, the image is the world's greatest healing resource. Imagery, or the stuff of the imagination, affects the body intimately on both seemingly mundane and profound levels."

When I discovered imagery, it became a lifelong quest to learn more and more about it. Not only did I use Achtenberg's work, but I also delved into any research I could find about imagery. Much of the research came from the sports field. This research found that when athletes added imagery to their physical practice, their performance improved. Research also taught me that imagery is most effective when it is multisensory. Later, I incorporated this into storytelling by using all the senses: visual, auditory, olfactory, touch, and gustatory.

I had tried out imagery with children, traveled to New York and Japan to imagery conferences, and read as many research studies as I could. In addition, I taught an undergraduate course in mysticism at Prescott College for six semesters, again honing my skills and observing students' reactions to imagery exercises.

I found a neuroscientist whose work struck me as a better fit than the right brain–left brain model for understanding how imagery could open the mind. Karl Pribram suggests that the limbic system may be involved in the expansion of perception. This structure includes the hypothalamus as well as the amygdala. The amygdala is one of my favorite human organs. It integrates sensory information and emotions, and it opens up long-term memory. For me, it is the perfect part of the brain to focus on with imagery. I coined Pribram's model "the middle brain" in my book, *Living the Wheel*.

In 1989, I published an article in the *Journal of the Society for Accelerative Learning and Teaching* on how the limbic system is involved in the cognitive process of learning. It is the part of the brain involved in storing and retrieving long-term memories, expanding one's field of perception, organizing sensory information, and regulating autonomic nervous system activity. The kicker was that imagery could access all these functions. When I moved into storytelling, I saw that storytelling could do the same.

During my imagery era, I delved into the cognitive processes of imagery across a wide-ranging continuum. From a strictly cognitive point of view, humans naturally think in imagery or pictures when they need to integrate a lot of information to solve problems. For example, engineers switch to thinking in images to solve complex tasks, as documented in Geir Kaufmann's book. Other psychologists examine the process of imagery with creativity. Many, like Paul Torrance, verified that creative insights come in visions. Geir Kaufmann, a psychologist at the University of Bergen, Norway, had written and done research showing that imagery is critical to creativity. When the mind has too much information to integrate, it moves to imagery, as in a picture is worth a million words. Also, many inventors and scientists report that their insights came in a vision. This fed into my growing confidence that imagery could transform consciousness.

Imagery and Creativity

In my book *Archetypal Imagery,* I showcase two famous scientists whose stories include vivid, spontaneous imagery. Nikola Tesla invented the alternating-current motor and developed alternating-current generation and transmission technology. People may know this name from the enormously popular electric car, the Tesla. His name was no doubt used because he was a genius inventor. Without his invention of the alternating-current motor, electricity could not be sent over long distances.

As a child, Tesla was very ill and bedridden. As a result, he created a life rich in imagery. He would actually design machines in his mind, test them, rotate them in 3D, and redesign them. He had many inventions. The story of how he invented the alternating-current motor is particularly stunning. He was in a park in Prague when, all of a sudden, he saw a blinding light in his field of vision, and the design came to him in a spontaneous image.

Another scientist with a vivid imagery story is Luigi Galvani. In 1780, Galvani, an Italian physician, discovered the electrical basis for nerve impulses. The story I've read is that he had a hunch and was trying to figure out the mechanism for the transmission of nerve impulses. As Galvani was falling asleep before a fire, he saw a mental image of an experiment in which he put frog legs in a petri dish and introduced an electrical charge. Humans have different brain waves. Beta accompanies an alert state. Alpha is an awake but relaxed state. Theta is a highly imagistic state that happens between waking and sleeping, and the delta state is deep sleep. Theta is the most creative, and that is what Galvani experienced. He did the experiment based on what he saw in his dream state, and "voila!" Scientific history was made by establishing that muscles move in response to an electrical charge.

Besides problem solving and creativity, I knew imagery accompanied an altered or expanded state of consciousness. My experience with yoga had created inner states of consciousness marked by bliss and a sense of interconnectedness with all life. This was in the late 1980s and early 1990s, when yoga, LSD trips, and transcendental meditation had permeated the U.S. baby boomer culture. That is one reason I wrote *Living the Wheel*. I wanted to communicate that one could be spiritual *and* emotional. Spiritual wasn't the same as being emotional. Sensing and transforming emotions worked conjointly with spiritual practice to clear the mind. I had found that imagery did this.

Imagery and Transformation of Emotions

In *Living the Wheel*, I document a technique that I learned at a 1987 imagery conference in Fukuoka, Japan, from Takeshi Masui. This involved visualizing an emotion in the body to release and transform it. The technique went like this: You think of a recent experience that evoked an emotion you didn't like. The scene where you felt the emotion is visualized in detail using as many senses as possible to vivify the experience. Then you find where the emotion is in your body. The key is to visualize the emotion in the body and not label the emotion or give meaning to it; just visualize it. You ask these questions: "Where is it? Is it in the stomach or the head? How big is it? Is it round or square? Does it have clear edges or amorphous edges?" After getting a clear image in the body, the next step in this process of transforming emotions is to change the visual of the image. This dissipates the emotional valence and allows you to clear your mind to see the emotion with perspective. Other questions could be: "Has the shape changed? Has the color? Does it feel better? What do I want to do about the situation now?" One of the assumptions of this work is that current emotions are tied to issues stored in the unconscious that have not been integrated. Current emotions are like a thread in a weaving that needs to be unwoven.

In *Living the Wheel*, my objective was to teach about the potential of imagery—how to use it to work with emotions and how to see imagery as a way to open and clear the mind. I hadn't yet developed quite what I thought about this as wisdom. That came later in my career.

I had kept my interest alive in helping children through research on different learning styles. I realized that some of the American Indian children had a strength in visual processing or imagery. During this time in my career in the late 1980s, I was doing research in imagery and presenting at international imagery conferences in Japan and New York City. I met a fellow psychologist from the UK, David Marks, who had published extensively on imagery. He asked me to place one of his students in a research practicum, Bisi Lalemi. We studied imagery training and creativity, which was published as "The Role of Imagery Training on Tohono O'odham Children's

Creativity Scores" in *the Journal of American Indian Education*. In this research, I wanted to add to the knowledge on imagery and creativity, as well as to showcase a possible strength of American Indian children: thinking in pictures or images. There was an experimental and a control group for children in second grade, aged eight, and sixth grade, aged twelve. The experimental group participated in six 15-minute imagery practice sessions, starting with improvisational rhythm to help evoke vivid imagery. Rhythm talks to the limbic systems of the brain, where the amygdala and the hypothalamus regulate rhythmic autonomic functions like blood pressure and heart rate. The part of the brain that mediates imagery, the limbic system, threading underneath the cerebral cortex, is rhythmic.

In addition to improvisational rhythm, the imagery session facilitator led them in a drawing activity. Students were given the figural form of the Torrance Test of Creative Thinking. Students who had the training improved on the creativity test, more than the control group—by 14 points—which is statistically significant.

After this study, I realized I wanted to work more with children, and I was excited about working cross-culturally. In the early 1990s, there were federal monies for substance abuse prevention because of Nancy Reagan's influence in the previous decade. Nancy, in her red dress, led the chorus: "Just say no!" As my study of imagery progressed, I realized that storytelling had the same effect on the mind as imagery. By 1990, I had worked on the Tohono O'odham Nation for four years, delivering a BA in education to tribal members who were teacher aides and had come to sense the importance of storytelling in tribal culture. One example is that elders told stories at night during the winter, tracing cosmology and also sharing the values of connection. I knew these experiences.

I learned so much during my study of imagery. I learned how powerful imagery was. Thinking in internal sensations could

- Increase T cells to combat disease
- Lower blood pressure and decrease heart rate
- Naturally open the memory banks and transit to the unconscious mind in a safe way to evoke memories that may need to be released or to evoke memories that could create joy

- Evoke states of expanded consciousness and a feeling of interconnection with other life
- Help a person experience uncomfortable emotions and transform them into emotional strength

Archetypes: Archetypal Identification Transforms Emotions

With my interest in imagery, it was hard not to think about archetypes. In Jungian psychology, archetypes are energy patterns in the collective unconscious that humans unconsciously align with or "live in front" of us to organize our personality. As adults, humans can consciously align with an archetype to open the unconscious, releasing emotional material that opens the mind towards spaciousness and wisdom. So, my knowledge was building. Yoga through a relaxed focus of attention creates awareness. Imagery also has a relaxed focus of attention and can calm the body. A connection to emotions can be released, and an opening to memory banks creates a permeable threshold to the unconscious. Most archetypes are personifications. Visualizing this archetype gives a safe way to open the unconscious and activates the psychodynamic of imagery.

The Invisible Dimension

I had begun to create a theory about how yoga, imagery, storytelling, and the main characters in stories—the archetypes—can transform a person's being. First, I needed to establish the assumption that opening the mind allows a person to access a dimension that taps into the wisdom humans have accumulated over time. There are different theoretical frames for understanding what this dimension is. One fundamental understanding across these theoretical frames is that it is outside of everyday consciousness. It is not part of the words in the mind that run through consciousness. A transformed being is in touch with deeper insight. In 1991, I held a conference called Native American Voices. I heard a Hopi man, Wil Numkena, explain that White people think the spirit world is up in the sky, but Hopis know that it is right beside us. It is an invisible domain that is accessible. I liked this a lot: an invisible domain we could sense right next to us.

The Hopi idea of an invisible dimension is similar to the energy field from Vedanta thought that I mentioned earlier. These two concepts also overlap with Jung's idea of the collective unconscious, which gives humans access to symbolic knowledge acquired over time. This is similar to humanistic psychologist Carl Rogers theory that there is a creative force in the unconscious that, when contacted, leads a person to healing and creativity. According to Rupert Sheldrake, a British biochemist, there is a morphogenetic field or an energetic field. When a species learns something, that learning is fed into this field. A chreode, or a valley, in this morphogenetic field is formed by a behavioral pattern of learning. Others of the same species can easily learn the same thing. To sum up these very different but similar core views, there is a space that human consciousness can touch if it is open enough to gain the knowledge that other humans have learned. It may not fit with everyone's view of reality that there is an energy field one can tap into for human wisdom. Even if this is not true, then opening the mind can still lead to wisdom. Since a relaxed mind can access processing usually outside of creativity, hidden memory, mental space, and conscious awareness, both rational and intuitive processes can solve problems and generate insight.

Yoga, imagery, and storytelling open the mind, and if it is done consistently over time, as practice, then consciousness is transformed. This allows a free flow of insight from the unconscious and possibly from the energy field, where the repository of human wisdom is stored.

Archetypes in Stories

As I continued to work with stories, I saw new layers of their effectiveness. Stories prompted identification with a character who served as an archetype. I thought that a human's identification with an archetype was a powerful key to the actual process of opening the mind-body to receive wisdom. I thought I could figure out what was happening with storytelling that could connect people with what

Joseph Campbell said were the "energies of the cosmos." Archetypes were a likely candidate, since according to Jung's personality theory, people naturally and unconsciously align with an archetype to organize their personalities.

The idea that archetypes are energy patterns that convey given characteristics can be extended beyond the basic three Jungian archetypes—the anima, animus, and shadow—there could be many more, such as an archetype of a teacher, a villain, or any pattern that conveys a given characteristic. Identifying with an archetype is a natural psychological process. According to Jung, identifying with an archetype is a natural psychodynamic. Archetypes reside in the collective unconscious, a spiritual dimension in which all life is interconnected. Children naturally and in an unconscious manner align with one to organize their personality. As adults, one can consciously choose an archetype to open the mind to release emotions and receive spiritual insight. Consciously aligning with an archetype relaxes the mind and softens the barrier between the conscious and unconscious mind.

Like the relaxed focus of attention in yoga, and seeing a picture in the mind like imagery, visualizing an archetype could do the same thing. But it can do even more, because since identification with archetypes is a natural psychodynamic, it can create a space to release emotional material trapped in the unconscious that prompts reactive responses and skewed perception. I wrote an article about it that was published in *The Humanistic Psychologist*, and I published *Archetypal Imagery,* in which I trained coaches and therapists to use this technique of finding and visualizing an archetype. They found it very effective. But I realized that it was too abstract to communicate effectively how archetypes could lead to wisdom. I decided that maybe telling stories was an indirect way, and that it wasn't necessary to spend too much time with archetypes. As the indigenous scholar Terry Tafoya says, stories plant symbols in listeners' minds that grow in meaning over time. The main characters in stories can be planted in people's minds. These main characters are archetypes. As a person hears a good story, they see scenes from the story and actually visualize them.

Archetypes are a powerful mechanism for making the barrier to the unconscious permeable, so in a psychologically safe manner, a person can have access to the unconscious. In the personal unconscious is a connection to the collective unconscious. Visualizing an archetype is a conduit to this dimension which contains human wisdom and relaxes and opens the mind for emotional authenticity and spiritual insight.

Storytelling: Bringing It Together

The *piece de resistance* is storytelling. It has a relaxed focus of attention; it has imagery of main characters and the main characters are archetypes. A focus of the mind allows space for emotions to come and go. Visualizing characters in stories that are archetypes opens the unconscious for clear perception and spiritual insight to emerge.

The benefits of yoga, imagery, and archetypal imagery came together for me in seeing storytelling as a vehicle to accomplish the same benefits as these practices. This happened when I worked on Indian Nations in Arizona, delivering a Bachelor of Arts with teacher certification for American Indian teacher aides to take over the classrooms of their schools. When I was an administrator at Prescott College, the Director of Education, Bernard Sequieros, from the Tohono O'odham (formerly Papago) Tribe, asked me to bring our external BA program to serve American Indian teacher aides. I was committed to bringing education to underserved populations. This was a thread in my life. My parents had instilled Christian values of loving others and helping the least among us, and had been models of working for civil rights. During college, I volunteered to teach reading to inner-city children. As a graduate student, I was a consultant for a program for Head Start graduates, training an educational model in low-income communities, including Indianapolis, Bronx, Philadelphia, Lame Deer, Hopis, and others. When I got to Prescott College, which was a primarily white institution, I wanted to help empower low-income students with education. The director of the Tohono O'odham Nation, southwest of Tucson, Arizona, contacted me and said, "Bring your BA program down here so that our

American Indian tribal member teacher aides can get their teaching credentials and take over the classrooms in a culturally affirming way." The call to set up a BA program for American Indian teacher aides was a gift.

Getting teacher aides from American Indian Nations with bachelor's degrees so that they could take over teaching jobs filled the bill. My colleagues and I adapted our external BA program to fit this need. This work immersed me in some of the cultures of the twenty-two American Indian tribes in Arizona. During my yoga era, I subscribed to *Yoga Journal*, which often features articles on shamans, and this gave me some perspectives on indigenous philosophy. Also, by learning from tribal education directors, I moved away from the Eurocentric hierarchical learning model that valued higher-order thinking, and I learned about circular models of wheels for balance and harmony in education. This opened up the world of using wheels as organizing tools, and I started studying wheels around the world. I created a multicultural learning model documented in *The Learning Wheel* (1998).

Working with indigenous views of learning took me back to the storytelling that I experienced as a child. My mother was a storyteller, so learning about indigenous storytelling was a double whammy for me as something of significance. Storytelling fitted my work with imagery because when listening to stories, people often see pictures in their minds of the characters, the scenes, and the action. My quest to find vehicles to move people toward wisdom led me to storytelling in a loving way. Besides prompting imagistic thinking, storytelling tapped into human wisdom. I saw storytelling as the access to Jung's collective unconscious. I saw the concept of the collective conscious as congruent with the Vedanta concept of the energy domain in the Hindu philosophy. Storytelling was connected to this stream of wisdom.

During the mid-1990s through the end of the first decade of the 2000s, I had started a non-profit called the WHEEL Council (Wholistic Health Education and Empowerment for Life), using storytelling as a main intervention tool for substance abuse and HIV prevention. Our curriculum was called the *Storytelling PowerBook.* I published articles showing positive outcomes for Tohono O'odham and Latina/Latino youth, and also used storytelling as an interviewing method to judge the effectiveness of youth development programs documented in a journal article. Through this research, I documented storytelling as a powerful tool for learning and emotional health, which are components of wisdom.

It is hard to overemphasize the role of stories in giving humans emotional stability. As Joseph Campbell says, stories tell us where we come from and where we are going. Stories from parents, grandmothers, grandfathers, aunts, and uncles give young people a sense of emotional safety. These stories ground people in a sense of generational place, not only their place in their family and cultural lineage, but also their place on the earth. Listening and thinking about stories is the foundation of understanding what it is to be a human. Cultural stories tell people about their natural relationship to the earth and others. The amazing thing about stories is that they develop self-knowledge as well as social and communal knowledge. Stories transmit information in a culturally sensitive and holistic manner and provide context. They are a fundamental, primitive, but evolving human form of communication.

Chapter Two: Wisdom

If storytelling is a vehicle for wisdom, then establishing the definition and qualities of wisdom is an important step in the journey. Paul Baltes and Ursula Staudinger talk a lot about wisdom in their *American Psychologist* article. They see wisdom as a combination of expert knowledge systems and fundamental pragmatics orchestrating knowledge with virtue. It is knowledge for the good of oneself and others. Wisdom is difficult to achieve but easily recognized. I will break it down in this chapter as much as I can break down an ineffable quality.

Wisdom Is Going Beyond and Through

> "Wisdom is a function of deep insight into, and mature understanding of, the central existential issues of life, together with practical skill in responding to these issues in ways that enhance the deep wellbeing."
> -Roger Walsh

Roger Walsh reiterates Aquinas's ideas that wisdom is both practical and esoteric, exploring existential philosophical questions about the meaning of life. Walsh has multiple doctorates in psychology, physiology, neuroscience, and medicine from Australia's Queensland University, and he is now a professor at the University of California, Irvine. He has been a circus acrobat and a wanna-be stand-up comedian. He obviously embraces a holistic, creative pursuit of life. Walsh has written extensively about spirituality and wisdom.

Walsh's writings add the concept of trans-conceptual to the definition of wisdom. "Trans" is a prefix meaning *beyond, across,* or *through.* "Trans-conceptual" means going beyond concepts to define wisdom. I like that idea of going beyond concepts. Not only does a person know something from a factual basis, but they also get the added spice of insight. Wisdom includes other ways of knowing, such as emotions, intuition, and spiritual insight. The wise person cultivates an inner space that allows connections between disparate elements to have "aha" moments. Wisdom is one of the most complex human capacities, which makes it hard to define.

Walsh's definition of wisdom and the experiences from my work with imagery led me to study shamanism. When shamans journey—fueled by drumming or psychedelic substances—they have visions that go beyond this world. Shamans from indigenous communities use drumming to evoke altered states of consciousness in which they find healing in visions. According to Mircea Eliade, a shaman is a member of a community who journeys to other worlds, either the sky world or the underworld, fueled by drumming, to bring healing back for their community. Manvir Singh supports this notion, saying a shaman enters a trance to provide service.

When I attended a Transpersonal Psychology Conference in 1984 at Asilomar Conference Center State Park on the beach near Monterey, California, a number of psychologists presented information about shamanism. The altered states of consciousness that shamans experience could be viewed as going beyond. In transpersonal psychology, people experience altered states of consciousness that are trans-conceptual, moving across and through logical concepts. Going beyond or experiencing a trans-conceptual state of consciousness is also found in Walsh's study of transpersonal psychology. This branch of psychology emerged in the late 1960s and built on humanistic psychologist Abraham Maslow's ideology about the human potential evident in peak experiences.

Abraham Maslow lived from 1907 to 1970. He created a hierarchy of needs that theorizes that as humans meet their basic needs in life, they move toward self-fulfillment and may eventually have peak experiences. Peak experiences are marked by love, understanding, happiness, and rapture. These culminate in a sense of inner connection with others and a commitment to altruism. He studied people he considered to be self-actualized, such as Albert Schweitzer.

Schweitzer was a doctor who committed his life to serving people in Africa and won a Nobel Peace Prize. Maslow judged him as being self-actualized.

By studying people like Schweitzer, Maslow developed his theory of human potential. Maslow broke with the field of psychology, which, up until then, had been focused on mental illness. As an extension of this, transpersonal psychologist Glenn Hartelius explored what occurred during these peak experiences, known as altered or expanded states of consciousness. The idea was to access states for spiritual awareness, emotional healing, creativity, and wellness. Yoga, meditation, prayers, and indigenous ceremonies held keys to this understanding.

Psychologists define "consciousness" as the inner experience that humans report. With meditation, prayer, joyous experiences in nature, feelings of love, or the expansive states of yoga, a person can experience alpha or theta waves that could calm and open the mind to wisdom.

Walsh uses the word "sagacity" frequently in his writings. I liked this term because people have an immediate sense when a person next to them is wise, or a sage. A sage is someone who emanates a certain quality. There is a sense of balance from a sage. The person not only knows facts but also experiential learning with a grounded sense of self melded with a spark of insight. The French have a saying describing people who are comfortable in their own skin: *être bien dans sa peau*. That is sagacity—a person who has become him- or herself.

The Children

Cultural stories showcase sagacity. *The Children* by Omoleye is based on a story from the Yoruba tribe of West Africa, which shows that being a sage combines experience, knowledge, and insight. This story takes place in a village in West Africa, home of the Yoruba near present-day Abidjan in Côte d'Ivoire. In the story, the village was a happy place, agrarian in nature with goats and ample root crops, including yams. The main characters are the families in the village and an elderly woman who lives outside the village. Elderly women often are featured in stories as embodying earth wisdom, and this is the case here.

Characters in stories undergo tests, and the main test in *The Children* is the ability of couples to conceive children, hence the story's name. It came about that the couples in the village could not conceive. Knowing the wisdom held by the elder, the villagers trooped to her house and implored her to solve their problem. The elder went into the jungle and collected several herbs, lit a fire, and used a large kettle to make a concoction. When it cooled, she took it back to the couples who had gathered. Soon fecundity began. Many couples conceived, and many had twins.

The villagers rejoiced and paid respect to the elder, going monthly to do repairs on her house or help her with gardening. This went on for many years, but as the children grew, the people forgot the elder, leaving her to her own devices. Then a new test was in store for the villagers, as their children became sick, and nothing they tried healed them. The villagers remembered the elder and went to see her again. Due to her infirmities, her house and gardens had gone into disrepair. The villagers pleaded with her to help them again, and again the elder went to the jungle, found herbs, and made a concoction for the parents to give their children. Lo and behold, the children were healed.

From that time forward, the villagers did not forget the elder, and they set up a system to go monthly to help her. The villagers learned a lesson about wisdom; it needs to be fed and nourished with practice. The elder in this story represents the wisdom of earth knowledge cultivated with experience and years of practice. Hearing and telling stories can become a way to keep wisdom alive.

The elder is an example of wisdom being trans-conceptual. The elder could see through the problem to heal the sick children. She went beyond her factual knowledge. She not only had the knowledge of what plants to use for what type of sickness, but also the experience and practice with their use. Here, inner balance allowed her to integrate all these ways of knowing into wisdom to heal the children.

Other Wisdom Teachers

Besides Walsh, two other spiritual teachers also refer to going beyond when explaining wisdom: Chögyam Trungpa and Joana Macy. Trungpa puts it like this: "Unerring insight into the true nature of phenomenon and of seeing through ego and its deceptions."

Trungpa was a Tibetan Buddhist teacher who came to the United States in 1970 and founded Naropa University in Boulder, Colorado. His life was marked by controversy due to his alcoholism later in life, but his books, such as *The Heart of the Buddha,* have great insight into wisdom. Tibetan Buddhism is known as the wisdom tradition. Trungpa said wisdom is seeing through our psychological makeup. There is more potential in the mind-body that is usually outside of our conscious awareness. A truism is that humans only use 10 percent of their brains. This is a simplistic view, but as a metaphor, it works that at any given time, humans are only using a small part of their minds' potential.

The chatter in human minds, with their storylines about identity and the need to shut out certain perceptions to navigate emotions, keeps humans from their inner wisdom. Wisdom is not only knowing facts and concepts or amassing experiential learning, but also being open to insight. To do this, a person needs an open mind to actually clearly perceive what is happening around the world in the present time.

Another Buddhist teacher and environmental activist, Joanna Macy, focused on wisdom as going beyond and through. Macy's story is inspiring. During her doctoral work, she studied with Huston Smith, who is the Joseph Campbell of comparative religion. Joseph Campbell studied stories and symbols from all over the world and found common themes. Smith did this for religions. Macy applied systems theory based on Gregory Bateson's work. Bateson, an English anthropologist who lived from 1904 to1980, was famous for developing systems theory, a theory that patterns in the mind work in an interdependent way. Thoughts are not independent of other patterns in the mind; they are part of interlocking systems.

Macy found similarities between Bateson's systems theory and Buddhism. As a result, she studied Theravada Buddhism, a Southeast

Asian tradition focusing on Buddha's original writings. Macy integrated systems theory, ecology, spirituality, and peace activism in her teaching and writing. I found her description of Prajna Paramita, a Buddhist deity, to be a very helpful archetype to elucidate wisdom. "Prajna Paramita" is translated from Sanskrit as "wisdom perfection." Macy writes, "Because she pointed to a reality which eludes classifications, this wisdom, *prajňa,* was called *paramita*, which means 'gone beyond' or to the 'other side,' as well as 'perfection,' she offered not theories but paradoxes."

I really like Prajna Paramita. First, I like that she is female. I always like it when a deity is female. I see the feminine divine as a metaphor for generating life as opposed to controlling life. It gives me hope, as a female, that I can grow toward wisdom. Secondly, I like the feminine view of creation that Paramita conveys. Macy calls Paramita "the pregnant zero" from which all reality originates. This certainly goes beyond facts and knowledge, and beyond the usual understanding of how the material world was created. The material world was spawned from the void by perfect wisdom.

I found a connection between Paramita's story and the story of Sophia, a Middle Eastern Deity. She is the creator in the Gnostic Gospels found in Egypt. I did a workshop for nurses on using imagery for healing. The main character of the story I made was Sophia. The name just came to me. People liked the story so much that I started researching who Sophia was. Marie-Louise von Franz, a Jungian therapist, called Sophia the self-knowing primordial cause or the energy from which "the archetypal world after whose likeness this sensible world was made." She also said that Sophia is the fundamental archetype, or the blueprint, of the material, sensible world. Sophia is derived from the Greek word *sophizesthai*, or "one who is wise." Her name is also derived from the Greek word *sophos*, or "to be of the same kind," possibly indicating that all life is of the same kind as Sophia, since she is the creator.

I personally worked with Sophia as my archetype, writing a story about her, finding anything written about her, and images of her. Attempting to embody Sophia helped me experience certain states of wisdom, moving beyond knowledge to a greater awareness.

The names Sophia and Prajna Paramita have a nice synchronicity. Jung defined synchronicity as two seemingly unrelated events occurring at the same time. But the two events are actually connected in a meaningful way. Synchronicity seems to be happening when the same idea pops into people's minds from the collective unconscious in different places at different times. In this case, Sophia and Prajna Paramita—even though from very different parts of the world, Egypt and Tibet—are both translated as "wisdom" and convey a similar creation story. This story is feminine in nature: There isn't a deity above making the world; rather, it is generated from the feminine spirit. In Tibetan sacred texts, Prajna Paramita is perfect wisdom, and in the Gnostic Dead Sea scrolls, the creator is Sophia.

The Dead Sea Scrolls story naming Sophia as the creator is unlike other creation stories. Usually, creation stories have a deity who acts to make the material world and all life. But in this story, the reality of the human world, the earth, and all life spring out of Sophia's being. Similar to Paramita personifying the pregnant zero, Sophia self-generates the ecosystems of Earth. Both Paramita and Sophia convey that wisdom is perceiving the essential nature of reality. To do this, a person needs to go beyond logic and knowledge to foster contact with the intangible elixir of insight.

Wisdom Is Emotional Balance

"Wisdom is a sense of friendliness or warmth not only
toward ourselves, but also toward the world."
-Chögyam Trungpa

People often think of wisdom as something that doesn't include normal day-to-day reality, but recall that Aquinas brought practicality into the mix. Wisdom is both practical and esoteric. Wisdom is perceiving reality as it is, and a person needs emotional balance to allow this to happen. Without emotional balance, the mind is filled with the chatter of internal storylines, the emotional vibrations of anxiety and fear, and the waves of perceptual details and sensations.

This internal noise prevents awareness from weaving together logic, knowledge, experience, and intuition.

There is a lot said about emotions in the twenty-first century, and "emotional intelligence" is a buzz term that is threaded through popular psychological literature. But the problem with this focus is the word "intelligence," which often refers to logical thinking. Emotions are not logical. "Emotional awareness" is a better term since it infers the ability to sense and release emotions instead of using logic to control them. With emotional balance, humans can think clearly.

Fritz Perls, who lived from 1893 to 1970, was a fellow humanistic psychologist to Maslow, and he had a practical dictum about emotions that, in my paraphrase, is "accept it to change it." This means emotional balance takes practice. The practice is to feel emotions authentically, sense them completely, and then allow them to change. Over time, this process can accelerate, allowing us to sense and release emotions more quickly, giving more space in the mind to integrate what is needed for wisdom. With space in our mind, we can perceive reality more clearly. The awareness of emotions is essential for this balance, so emotions do not take over conscious awareness. With awareness, we can notice an emotion and then release it.

Emotional reactive patterns in the unconscious will run the mind unless they are released. To Jung, a person becomes fully human by releasing material in the mind's shadow. Jung says the unconscious will run the mind unless the mind runs it. The shadow is what people don't know or reject about themselves. Some of this unknown material may be positive, also known as the golden shadow. People sometimes are unaware or are shut off from their gifts, and they often have a skewed perception of themselves. Also, of course, in the shadow are some negative things, difficult or painful memories, or maladaptive views of the self. Opening the shadow releases this material and clears more mind space, allowing people to perceive reality without inner interference. When this is done, a person is no longer controlled by blocks in the unconscious.

To be wise is to become oneself, becoming fully human by opening the shadow to create space in the mind. This creates emotional balance. The great Vedanta yogi, Patanjali, said that emotions are like clouds and storms blowing through the mind, revealing a clear, blue sky. Patanjali, a sage in Hinduism, lived between the second and fourth centuries BCE, and he is thought to be the author of the *Yoga Sutras,* which document the practice and theory of yoga from oral traditions and offer foundational information on yoga philosophy.

The Dragon's Robe

The Dragon's Robe, retold by Deborah Lattimore, shows that emotional balance prompts wisdom. This is the Chinese story of Kwan Yin. Kwan Yin is the Chinese form of Avalokiteśvara, who is the Buddha of compassion in Tibetan Buddhism. The Dalai Lama is said to be an incarnation of Avalokiteśvara. Kwan Yin is a young woman in this story, and her name has significance. Herein, Kwan Yin relies on emotional balance amid adversity.

There was a great famine in China. Kwan Yin was a weaver caught in adversity. She was all alone, as her parents had died. She had heard that within three days, the Emperor would choose a robe to wear, and he would reward the weaver of this robe with a lifetime job. Kwan Yin was determined to be that weaver, and she started the long journey from her village to Beijing. She had to cross over mountains through a desiccated landscape, and she grew faint with hunger. She came to a small house and went inside to see whether there was water. She found an Old Man lying on a cot who was in a very weak state. She found water and helped him drink. He told her he was in charge of the Dragon Shrine nearby and asked her to help him tend to it until he was well. She initially protested, since she was on her way to the Emperor's weaving competition, but she soon relented.

Kwan Yin kept weaving, as she always carried her loom with her, even amid the tasks of tending to the shrine. She was weaving a robe of fine silk for the Emperor. The Old Man gave her golden bamboo shoots to put on the altar. Just as she was on the way to the altar, Lord Phoenix came riding through. He, too, said he would help place the shoots on the altar. The Old Man asked her to watch him to see what he did. As she watched, Lord Phoenix decided to take the bamboo shoots for his own. Kwan Yin reported this to the Old Man, and immediately, a great wind came and ruined all the rice fields within miles.

The next day, another Lord came. This one was Lord Tiger. He, too, said he would help tend the temple, and he helped Kwan Yin place a golden dagger on the altar. Again, Kwan Yin was instructed to watch what the Lord did, and as with Lord Phoenix, Lord Tiger decided to rob the shrine. He took the golden dagger for himself. As he did, the Khan's army surged over the Great Wall and wreaked havoc as they invaded China.

During all this, Kwan Yin kept her head and kept weaving the garment she planned to give to the Emperor, even as the rice fields burned and Khan's armies invaded. She shot weft through the warp as the world erupted in chaos around her. Finally, the robe was done. She took it off the loom and showed it to the Old Man. A miraculous thing happened as he put the robe on. He became the Emperor, standing tall in the robe that was fittingly emblazoned with a dragon on the back. As the Emperor's power was restored, Khan was vanquished, and the rice fields grew again. Kwan Yin and the Emperor traveled to Beijing, where she was awarded the prize, joining his court.

Kwan Yin showed great emotional balance in this story. Regardless of what happened around her, she kept weaving. Without emotional balance, Kwan Yin could not have withstood the pressure and demands, and she would have been deterred from her role as the humble weaver. Kwan Yin had something to focus on, which allowed her to maintain her presence and awareness. It is important to note that a practice of some sort—in this case, the eye-hand focus of weaving—gave her balance. Other practices such as mindfulness, meditation, or yoga also help develop emotional balance.

Wisdom Is Spiritual

"Knowledge is transformed into wisdom
by means of compassion."
-Chögyam Trungpa

I mentioned Chögyam Trungpa earlier in the definition of wisdom. He lived from 1939 to 1987. He introduced Vajrayana Buddhist teaching to the West. Vajrayana is one of the three main Buddhist teaching traditions. The others are Theravada (the teaching of elders) and Mahayana (insight through meditation). As I mentioned, I found his book, *The Heart of the Buddha*, foundational in defining wisdom. It was similar to an experience that I had in Japan. I was meditating in a Buddhist temple, and I had an experience of my heart splitting in joy as I was filled with the compassion of the heart of the Buddha. As I sat crying, a monk came and gave me a Kleenex as if this were a normal event.

Trungpa's quote that compassion is what changes knowledge into wisdom suggests that a major life event is needed to awaken a human's empathy as the catalyst. Stories of deities that emanate spirituality show that traumatic experiences awaken the compassion of transformation. Similarly, all heroes and heroines face tests in stories. The ability to perceive what is, as opposed to what one thinks, is actually wisdom. This may sound overly simplistic, but it is quite complex. Swami Rama and others define the Vedanta model of the mind while noting several divisions. The model explains why the mind can't perceive reality as it is. There is a division called mind stuff, which is the thoughts that cycle in the mind. Then there is the sensory memory mind, which floods consciousness with perceptions and feelings.

Besides this division, there are also long-term memories tinged with emotions that can erupt. All this mental activity keeps a person from perceiving what is actually happening outside and inside oneself. But there is hope. In this view, when the mind is quieted, awareness naturally contacts the *buddhi,* the wisdom faculty. It is a nice paradox that once the mind is transformed, then wisdom comes naturally.

The Blind Men and the Elephant

With practice, awareness becomes clear, allowing the perception of reality as it is. The story of *The Blind Men and the Elephant,* retold by John Saxe, shows this clearly. This story goes that six blind men are brought to an elephant without being told what it is, and are asked what it is. They each touch a different part of the elephant, and report what they feel.

- The elephant's side, a "wall"
- The elephant's tusk: a "spear"
- The elephant's ears, a "fan"
- The elephant's tail, a "rope"
- The elephant's trunk, a "snake"
- The elephant's leg, a "tree"

Not one could perceive the essence of the elephant by touching only a part.

Each blind man has a piece of reality, but none of them has the gestalt of the elephant, the whole. Like the blind men, most people have a limited perception of reality, with emotions rolling through, and energy trapped in the unconscious. A relaxed, focused practice, such as telling and listening to stories, opens the mind. It gives a point of stability that lets emotions come and go, de-triggering reactive responses, and over time, the barrier to the unconscious becomes permeable, naturally releasing unconscious material. A spacious mind allows clear perception and rational thought, intuition, and spiritual insight.

If people are wise, then they can sense the true nature of reality, as the blind men in the Indian story could not. The mind opens to perceive through expanded consciousness. Perceiving reality as it is can sometimes be a surprise; it can be something one does not suspect. It can be deeper and wider than one thought. Just as the six blind man couldn't figure out what the elephant was in actuality, others can't perceive reality as it is unless they open their minds to wisdom. Stories conveying deep wisdom can do this.

Wisdom Is Creative

"It should be regarded as a higher-level thought process that

goes beyond the logical, rational processes, and one that can be enhanced by practice and instruction that encourages higher states of consciousness beyond the logical, wakeful state; combines intellectual, volitional, and emotional function."
-Mary Murdock

Humans certainly think in many ways, but one simple lens to understand cognitive modes is what psychologists call *convergent* and *divergent* thinking. These words are self-defining. Convergent thought zeroes in on a specific idea. Divergent thought allows a lot of ideas at once. Creativity is defined as combining ideas in a new way, and convergent thought initially doesn't allow this since the mind is drilling down on some specificity. However, when divergent ideas that seem unrelated are allowed in the mental mix, they could coalesce into a new way of looking at things over time.

For example, brainstorming relies on divergent thinking. It is a group process, where there is a task or problem proposed, and the group is asked for ideas, no matter how silly or "off the wall" they may seem. Entertaining any idea, even though it seems silly, is encouraged. Mind mapping is another technique to foster creative thinking. Ideas are put down on paper and connected with circles or lines instead of making a linear outline. I use mind mapping with my doctoral students to help them integrate ideas before they write scholarly papers.

Circling back to wisdom, the transformation of the inner world to be spacious and open allows divergence. This inner calm inside gives space so that a new idea can pop up that helps us look at an issue, a problem, or an event in a new way for insight and directions.

Wisdom Is Paradoxical

"The paradox is one of our most valued spiritual possessions."
-C.G. Jung

In Jungian psychology, the tension of opposites propels growth. C.G. Jung, living in the late nineteenth century and into the twentieth century, was a Swiss psychologist who worked in hospitals with schizophrenics. He noticed patterns in his patients' dreams and delusions. He studied with Freud until he attempted to analyze Freud's dreams on a transatlantic boat trip. Freud did not take kindly to this. A rift developed, but Jung went on to break with Freud's theory and develop his own theory of the collective unconscious, tracing symbols across human consciousness through his patients' dreams. Jung put the unconscious in a positive light. This was counter to Freud's view that the unconscious was the domain of the primitive id. In Jung's theory, a person can become individuated and free from inner and external influences by opening the shadow in the unconscious. Awareness is then also open to information from the collective unconscious. Jung's theory defines the Self as the whole of the person's inner world.

As mentioned earlier, Jung's basic archetypes are the anima (the feminine side), the animus (the masculine side) plus the shadow. Each person has both anima and animus, setting the stage for a paradox in psychodynamic development. Bringing awareness to both energies creates a transformation that transcends dualism. It is not either/or but a synthesis of something new. Wisdom is the ability to allow the mind to ponder opposites simultaneously, and this tension allows insight to come. Paradox, or the tension of opposites, acts to transform consciousness since the mind must relax to resolve the opposites.

A common representation of the power of paradox is the Tao. In my book, *Archetypal Imagery,* I use the Tao as an example of how paradoxical thinking is a form of wisdom. The Tao comes from the sixth-century BCE text, *Tao Te Ching,* by sage Lao Tzu. This book provides the basics of ancient Chinese philosophy, Taoism, for creating a balanced life in harmony with nature. Paradox is at the core of this philosophy—for example, Lao Tzu wrote, "What is and what is not create each other." By aligning with nature, which is full of paradoxes, one can expand the mind. Opposites are allowed in the mind at the same time, and as Jung says, the tension creates something new. Resolving paradoxes can create wisdom by making the mind agile.

Paradox is beyond logic; it goes through and beyond as in the definition of wisdom. It does not mean that one is illogical. There is logic, and there is more. In terms of the Tao, people often see the teaching as jumping between opposites: male and female, white and black, nature and humans. However, paradoxical thinking allows both to exist and can prompt a new combination of ideas. Wisdom is needed to navigate the seemingly different needs of the opposite, such as human civilization and the protection of Earth's ecosystems. A mind that can allow both of these to exist at the same time may find the path through. Paradoxical thinking is not compromising between the two opposites but rather holding the opposites at the same time to prompt a new insight to form.

I am a Zen Buddhist practitioner. The Heart Sutra is something we chant before sitting. "Sitting" is the name of meditation in Zen. Sitting has helped my understanding of paradox by reading Shunryu Suzuki's book, *Zen Mind, Beginner's Mind*. He was a famous Zen *roshi*, a teacher who has received dharma transmission from another roshi. Dharma is the teachings of the Buddha. Suzuki founded the first Buddhist monastery outside Japan, the Tassajara Zen Mountain Center, and also the San Francisco Zen Center. In Zen, paradox is also called non-dualistic thinking. Instead of thinking in opposites and deciding that one concept is correct and its opposite is incorrect, non-dualism allows both to exist.

The Heart Sutra

A section from the Buddhist Heart Sutra illustrates the power of paradox. Notice Paramita makes another appearance in the tales of wisdom.

No eye, ear, nose, tongue, body, mind.
No color, sound, smell, taste, touch, object of thought
No seeing and so on to no thinking,
No ignorance and also no ending of ignorance
And so on to no old age and death
And also no ending of old age and death;
No anguish, cause of anguish, cessation, path;
No wisdom and no attainment

One of my students, Megumi Sugihara, did her research on non-dual global justice activists. She had been an activist for food justice, possibly one of those demonstrators at a G8 meeting yelling at multinational corporations and the World Bank. At one point in her work, she decided that she had been going about it wrong. She had been thinking in terms of opposites. For example, the leftist green liberal demonstrators were good, and the corporate multinationals and banks were bad. In her new view, effective change might come from non-dualistic thinking. In her research, she interviewed eight activists whom she considered non-dual thinkers. Some worked with NGOs, some were authors, and some were spiritual teachers. All worked on environmental action and other social change issues. They reported non-dual consciousness, or not making judgments about ideas being wrong or right. Instead of working against a group that they thought was wrong, they worked for a unifying vision— the outcome of paradoxical thinking.

These activists reported that a conceptual understanding alone was not enough, even though understanding economic globalization and inequality was necessary for action. They needed to transform their own consciousness to be effective workers and to see the interconnection with others. Part of their activism was helping others transform consciousness. Megumi's study showed that wisdom from non-dualistic thinking could help people become agents for solving intractable social problems.

Wisdom Is Inter-individual

"The most difficult transformation as we move into this new paradigm is the realization of an interiorized spirituality."

"The Goddess is the unspeakable wisdom that grows into the very cells of the body, the beauty and the horror of the whole of life are blazing in Her love."
-Marion Woodman and Elinor Dickson

In Woodman and Dickson's book, *Dancing in the Flames: The Dark Goddess in the Transformation of Consciousness*, the authors review the evolution of paradigms for human society. They describe the transitions of the paradigms. The first paradigm was matriarchal, in which life was valued and dependence on others was the theme. The second was patriarchal in which organization was valued and control was the theme. They speculate that humans could move into an androgynous paradigm where interdependence is valued, and spirituality is the theme.

Karen Palamos also writes about humans evolving to an eco-psychological consciousness. She says that humans' sense of interconnectivity with all life will prompt them to become agents of change. Joanna Macy coined the phrase "the greening of the self" to help us re-inhabit our story with the awareness of interconnection in daily life.

Marion Woodman, a paragon in the world of Jungian thought, died in 2018 at the age of 89. She was a Canadian analytical psychologist and furthered the work of Jung with a feminist psychology lens. I wrote to her once, and she wrote me back. I've always treasured her letter. As a young woman, she was anorexic and traveled to India and England, finally enrolling in the C.G. Jung Institute in Zurich. Two of her books had a huge impact on me. One was *The Ravaged Bridegroom*. I loved the title since it was so evocative and visceral. What I liked about Jungian thought was that it did not shy away from the pain and the dark in life, but simultaneously is marked by hope. By opening the shadow in the unconscious, the difficulty can be brought to conscious awareness and then released. Sensing the whole of the inner world, called the Self, accelerates development toward full potential. Also, opening the inner world allows other aspects of one's character to balance with more maladaptive ones. Perspective and balance emerge. Once, I heard a Jungian analyst explain Jung's view of the Self. The human path for growth is to open the unconscious of all the elements of a person's character, the positive elements and the negative ones. He called this the mandala of the Self.

I'm not sure I learned that much from Woodman's *The Ravaged Bridegroom*, but I did from her next book. My eldest daughter, McCoy, bought me Woodman and Dickson's *Dancing in the Flames*. I'm not a Jungian analyst, even though Jungian thought is a home for me in terms of the transformation of consciousness. I think I've found a way to use the theory to see a natural way to change the topography of the inner world toward wisdom. I don't connect with the detailed dream analyses in books like Woodman's, nor the focus on Roman or Greek gods and goddesses archetypes. But I liked Woodman and Dickson's view of the evolution of consciousness to androgyny, interdependence, and spirituality.

Earlier, I documented that wisdom is going beyond and through; this allows humans to feel interconnection with other life. Woodman and Dickson define the primary quality of the androgynous paradigm as interconnection and awareness of the importance of nature. A wise person's mind is open to sensing one's interconnection with nature, which in turn could help protect Earth's ecosystems.

Another author I call on for using interconnection as a quality of wisdom is Robert Kegan. Kegan, a famous Harvard psychologist, is a prolific writer and theoretician of adult learning. From my background with a PhD in developmental psychology, I see Kegan in the tradition of others like Jean Piaget. These theorists propose stages that humans move through in their development as they interact with the environment. For example, Piaget traced a child's cognitive development from the age of twelve, from reacting to sensations to making logical deductions. Piaget's theory stopped at age twelve, but Kegan created a spectrum of development over a lifetime. He not only included cognitive abilities but also spiritual and emotional development. His last stage is inter-individual, which is similar to interconnectivity from Woodman, Macy, and Karen Palamos' work. Kegan's book *In Over Our Heads* creates a theoretical model for this development. As the title implies, the last stage may be defined as beyond and through.

Qualities of Wisdom

Becoming wise is a natural developmental state for humans. For psychologists, it is Kegan's inter-individual state when a person senses the interconnection with other life. People who have transformed consciousness into wisdom are agile and flexible in their inner world. They may have qualities of creativity, spirituality, and emotional balance. This doesn't mean that they are emotionless, but rather they can feel strong emotions and then return to a balance as the emotions are sensed and then released like clouds blow through the sky. They also may have the ability to think in paradoxes and trans-conceptually to see beyond by adding insight to facts and experience. My quest as a seeker of the techniques to help humans naturally transform consciousness to wisdom led me to storytelling.

Chapter Three: Storytelling

"Stories present deep insights into the affective dimension of human learning, socialization in community, and the role of story in the transfer of cultural knowledge and values… The deep psychological mechanisms associated with myths, stories, and storytelling facilitate the development of not only self-knowledge but also social and communal knowledge on the part of children…"

"Story is one of the most basic ways that the human brain structure relates human experience. Everything that humans do and experience revolves around some kind of story."
-Gregory Cajete

My love for storytelling goes back many, many years. This love was engendered around the time I was three, when my mother told me stories and read me books. As I mentioned in my journey, she was a drama and speech teacher, and as such, she had a lot of verve in her reading that merged with the oral tradition of storytelling. She would do readings for women's clubs, putting on big hats and dressing in period costumes. I was a bit embarrassed by her showmanship as she knew no bounds in her enthusiasm. From my perspective, she often overacted. But she was effective, and she modeled for me a pattern for communicating to others to entice imagination and move minds into the mythic realm of story.

There is one picture of my mom that stands out in my mind. She was standing in front of our home in Kansas City, Missouri, a 1920s house built of sandstone from the sediment laid down millions of years ago in the riverbeds of North America's heartland. It had a stone wall to support our large front yard with huge maples. I could watch the comings and goings on the street from that wall. Sometimes I sneaked out of the upper windows onto the porch roof and enjoyed the wind in the rustling maple leaves. I loved our house. As a little girl, I would Hulu-Hoop outside while watching for the milkman. My best friend Jerry, who lived across the street, and I would sneak into his truck to steal some of the crushed ice used to keep the milk bottles cold.

My feelings for the house put a nostalgic frame around this photo of my mom tinged with love. In the picture, she has a big straw hat on and a fake braid. She wore a dress with a cinched waist. She was on her way to a women's club to tell a story. I don't remember what story, but it was an iconic photo of my mom as a storyteller. My nonprofit, the WHEEL Council, had storytelling conferences over the years. I felt that I was metaphorically putting on my mother's big hat.

I don't really remember her reading stories to me, but we trekked to the library once a week to get books. I was able to read when I was four, and I'm not sure who taught me, probably my older, loving sister, Linda. I loved historical fiction about poor women who became queens or such. I remember reading a green book titled *Told Under the Green Umbrella*, published by the Literature Committee, and I still have it. I've seen it on sale on Amazon for $768, so I'm glad I saved my mother's copy. One of my favorite stories was *The Princess on the Glass Hill*. It is about Cinderlad, which I will share later.

As my path evolved to find the techniques to open the mind to wisdom, my work with American Indian Nations in Arizona became quite significant in leading me to storytelling. As mentioned earlier, I worked with the twenty-one Indian Nations in Arizona to deliver a teacher education program to help teacher aides become certified. In my work in schools on the Nations, I experienced elders passing on the storytelling tradition in their tribes. I realized that storytelling had the same cognitive effect as imagery. When people hear stories, they see pictures in their minds of the characters and the scenes. This was my re-entry into storytelling after being raised by a storytelling mother. Based on my work with imagery, I realized that storytelling could have powerful effects on the inner world. Later, I realized that hearing stories, telling stories, and creating stories could be a path to the transformation of consciousness that leads to wisdom.

Looking at the role stories play in indigenous societies offers clues to the ancient wisdom they convey. I spent fourteen years working with CIBTE. Over the years, young White teachers came to get teaching jobs on the Nations. There was a high turnover of non-tribal teachers. Even though well-intentioned, young White teachers weren't versed in local cultural values. However, tribal members were serving as teacher aides who did not have teaching credentials.

Tohono O'odham teacher aides had many hours of low-division credit but could not get bachelor's degrees and teaching credentials while living on the Nation. Prescott College could deliver this, and so began the work that immersed me in indigenous storytelling traditions. I adapted the adult degree program for Tohono O'odham and other tribes. I also worked with the Arizona Department of Education to have our BA education degrees approved, and we graduated hundreds of teacher aides with teaching credentials.

Tohono O'odham translates to "desert people." The Spanish had named them *Papago*, which meant "bean eaters." The O'odham have a rich cultural tradition, being famous as basket weavers. Their stories celebrated the cosmology of I'itoi, the creator, who lived in a cave near the top of the Baboquivari, a peak nearly 8,000 feet high, arising from the high desert of saguaro, mesquite, and Palo Verde trees. There is a famous symbol of I'itoi in the middle of a circular maze. The circle is so important in indigenous thought and storytelling, showing the cycle of life and how to become wise. The circle symbolizes the circular route to come to the middle of the maze.

Working on the Tohono O'odham Nation, I learned the power of storytelling to evoke vivid images similar to what happens when engaging in imagery activities. I'd discovered that an internal focus on a specific image, such as the characters in a story, was the way to open the mind to transform consciousness into wisdom.

Through the work of setting up a program for tribal members, I became fascinated by indigenous cosmology. In European and U.S. psychology, human development is usually viewed as a hierarchical endeavor. There are stages in development, and a person moves from one to the next. But the indigenous view is more holistic. Development is not like going up a ladder but going inward for balance and harmony. This jives nicely with Jungian theory—that human development is opening the inner shadow to awareness of the whole Self.

Wheels for Balance and Harmony

Stories tell of the circular nature of life. One might see stories in concentric rings. Concentric rings show the inter-relationships of the natural world of ecosystems, animals, plants, rocks, rivers, and lakes as these connect with family, cultural, and societal life. Rings are a symbol of wholeness and a visual symbol of how each element of the ring is interconnected.

The circle is the organizing principle in story to understand one's life on the planet and in the cosmos and to align natural and cosmological forces for balance and harmony. The circle represents unity metaphorically as the path of the sun and moon, the nest of a bird, or the interdependence of all forms of life in the cycle of life and death. Strength comes from working circularly as infinity without a beginning or end.

As I studied storytelling, I learned that balance and harmony are represented in wheels or circles in indigenous cosmology. I spent many years studying wheels around the world, from Scottish Celtic sources to Gandhi's wheel for creating a healthy democratic society to the North American Lakota medicine wheels. I documented this research in my book *The Learning Wheel*. Wheels are usually oriented toward the four directions. For a person to create balance and harmony within the self, all four directions, or energies, need to be attended to. This expanded my concept of the transformation of consciousness from experiencing transcendent visions to becoming whole within oneself. For example, in the Lakota wheel, documented in Hyemeyohsts Storm's *Seven Arrows,* a person associates with people who personify the different energies of the wheel and thereby becomes balanced.

During my work with Prescott College, I was motivated to create an excellent higher education program for the tribal members who were teacher aides. I needed to learn this because I was a product of excellent higher education under a Western model. Logic, higher-order thinking, science, math, and critical analysis were the keys in this system. However, I was also encultured by my mother to work for social justice. I wanted to make the program work.

My PhD program helped me understand learning theory and how to create effective learning environments. Much of my expertise came from behavioral psychology, which is criticized by many as being reductionistic. The criticism is that human learning is more than responding to consequences. But the strength of behavioral psychology is that it is very pragmatic. As a curriculum developer, I designed environments that were learner-centered. The learner was never wrong, which always meant starting with the learner.

When I first began designing the program, I thought I would build bridges between Prescott College and the tribal communities we were serving. But I soon discovered that the idea of building a bridge was a Western cultural idea, a logical deduction. At the same time, I knew we had to set up programs that affirmed and responded to the learners' lives that included their culture. I convened a meeting in Prescott with the directors of education from the Hopi, Navajo, Apache, and Hualapai tribes. I led the directors in an exercise of creating the perfect college experience for members of their tribes. What I heard was not what I expected nor what I thought was a college education.

The director of the Hopi tribe told me the metaphor of the planting stick. In this story, a young boy learns from his grandfather how to use a planting stick. The grandfather takes the boy out into the dry farming field. The Hopi Nation is located in an arid and dry environment, from 5,000 to 7,000 feet of elevation, with grasslands and a pinyon and juniper forest. The Hopis have lived on the mesas in Northern Arizona for three millennia and have perfected dry farming to grow blue corn. In the story, the grandfather asks the boy to watch without asking questions as he uses the planting stick. The grandfather demonstrates using the stick to dig a deep hole, plant the kernel of corn, and then cover it with sand. Without talking, the grandfather gestures for the boy to imitate the model. This is a basic learning strategy: model and imitation. This approach didn't seem like higher education to me. It went against the higher-order thinking skills and open-ended questions. However, I knew there was truth there. If one saw learning as a wheel, then the planting stick metaphor was a necessary point on the wheel. College education didn't need to be the only way I had been taught; there were other ways of learning.

During the years I worked with tribes, I immersed myself in American Indian history, writing, research, and publications. One book by Russell Thornton, *American Indian Holocaust and Survival: A Population History 1492,* opened my eyes to the effects of European colonization in North America—a holocaust. Thorton writes, "The American Indian population in the United States decreased from 5+ million in 1492 to 250,000 in the decade from 1890–1900."

One effective genocidal method was that the White settlers were given bounties to kill buffalo as train tracks were laid across the continent. They shot the buffalo from the trains. Without a food source, the Plains Indians were forced to submit to treaties and relocation.

Another source in my re-education of U.S. history was a journal produced by Cornell University in Ithaca, New York. The university had a strong American Indian center and published a journal titled *Northeast Indian Quarterly.* Situated in New York, the journal was influenced by the Haudenosaunee. This is the traditional name of the Iroquois Confederacy who were named by the French from a derivation of the word "snake." The Haudenosaunee (translated as the long house confederacy) were five and then six nations: Seneca, Cayuga, Onondaga, Oneida, Mohawk, and Tuscarora. Benjamin Franklin learned of the government of the confederacy as he designed the structure of the United States. One article I particularly liked was the documentation of the Dutch buying Manhattan Island in 1626. The Dutch had a contract for the Haudenosaunee to sign, and the Haudenosaunee brought a wampum belt, which symbolized that the two peoples would be brothers forever. Obviously, the two cultures had different ways of knowing. One was rational, and one was metaphoric.

Working with indigenous epistemologies led me to find and learn about wheels. In Western learning theory, education is hierarchical. In Bloom's taxonomy of learning, which most educators are taught in school, learning is organized in levels from simple to more complex. Literal learning, as in memorizing facts, is at the bottom, and more complex forms of learning move up a ladder to evaluative learning, where one can make conclusions. Another way of creating an education system is to use a wheel, where different ways of knowing are at the same level.

One wheel I discovered was the Kalachakra, a Tibetan ceremonial calendar that symbolizes the impermanence of time. Tibetan monks often create the Kalachakra out of sand and then sweep it aside. Another I found was the Aztec stone calendar; it was used extensively as a symbol of Mexico. This wheel depicts the cosmos: the Sun in the middle and the four elements of earth, wind, fire, and water are around it. I was living in Arizona at the time of this research, and I found the Diné wheel documented by Herbert Benally. It emphasizes the four seasons of the year and the tribal creation story. Learning about wheels, of course, enhanced my work on the Diné Nation with the Prescott College program. Diné means "the people." The Spanish called them Navajo. The Diné is the second largest tribe in the U.S., and the reservation is located in the Four Corners area—the states of Arizona, New Mexico, Utah, and Colorado. In the Diné wheel, the four directions are making a living, thinking and planning, physical and spiritual harmony, and life values. In the middle of the wheel is a convergence—where "to know" and "to love" are the same.

Of course, one of the more famous wheels is the Lakota medicine wheel. As documented in Hyemeyohsts Storm's *Seven Arrows*, each of the directions is different, signified by a unique color and an animal. In Storm's Lakota wheel, the four points are not only an animal but also different energies: illumination, innocence, introspection, and wisdom. These four energies are important to develop to a whole and balanced person.

As an organizing tool, there are some basic concepts about wheels, always using multiples of four. Wheels are used to align with the creative energies of the earth to bring wisdom and, as such, have four points of cardinal directions. Notably, the wheels are about wholeness, not achievement. This is an indigenous change from a Eurocentric notion of development: getting better and higher. The center of this wheel mirrors Chögyam Trungpa's definition of wisdom, that wisdom is knowledge touched by compassion.

Each point of the wheel holds a specific energy, and each needs to be addressed for wholeness and to actualize potential. According to Storm, a person needs to attend to each energy around the wheel to be a whole and balanced person. When I visited an ashram in Ahmedabad, Gujarat, India, I found Gandhi's wheel. Of course, I had revered Gandhi, and I was teaching on a Fulbright in the state of Gujarat. It was Gandhi's home state. He said he would stay there until India was free of the colonial rule of Britain. My family and I traveled from the small town in India where I taught. As I entered the ashram, I felt total reverence when going into the museum that was his ashram. When I went to the small room that was his bedroom, I noticed the pallet on the floor and his loom beside it. Gandhi's symbol of India's independence was the loom, representing that Indians could take back the production of fabrics from the British colonizers for economic independence.

When I saw a poster on the wall above his bed, I was struck with awe. It was a wheel. Gandhi had used a wheel to show the elements of a just and democratic society. Truth and nonviolence were in the middle of the wheel. As indigenous tribes of North America had found the organizing system of the wheel to be a way to move to wholeness, Gandhi had used the wheel as well. This was an omen for me that I should pay attention to wheels.

I collected wheels from around the world. Of course, people are criticized for cultural appropriation, as they should be. Working with American Indian Nations, I was sensitive to this. In the Hopi Nation, there are three main mesas with ancient pueblos. During the hippie era, young White people would come to the Nation to find their spiritual purpose, and they camped where they weren't wanted. I didn't want to contribute to this. I had the sense that wheels had been used around the planet. After all, wheels were designed to align human activity with cosmology to the four directions, the energy that keeps the earth in its orbit. If one could align human activities to the creative forces that kept the earth on its orbit, then there could be power and creativity in the human endeavor.

I found a wheel in Scotland, created as a geographic game board that the Celtic king would use to visit his lands. I found a wheel in Africa that a Yoruba elder used in healing ceremonies. Since wheels were found in global cultures for organizing ceremonies, government systems, and astrology, I thought I was on safe ground to write about them and use them.

For *The Learning Wheel,* I integrated what I knew about learning in behavioral psychology and about imagery and transformation of consciousness for creativity. This created my learning wheel of practical, technical, conceptual, creative, and expanded intelligence. I was excited and thought that if teachers could use this wheel to create lesson plans, then they could reach students from different ethnicities and cultures that might nurture different ways of knowing. A visual model of these intelligences would not be a hierarchy since no intelligence is more important than another. A circle would be more appropriate for showing the interrelationship of all intelligences.

My wheel rests on the premise that intelligence is culturally relative and that different cultures support different ways of knowing. There are four intelligences around my learning wheel with expanded intelligence in the middle. I took this idea from the Diné wheel, where there is energy in the middle. I wanted to make sure that my multicultural intelligence model included what I knew about opening the mind to more potential through non-rational knowing. Non-rational knowing is that which doesn't use linear processing, as in the left brain–right brain model. Non-rational knowing is metaphoric, visual, and kinesthetic. It is important in opening up memory, creativity, and insight. Therefore, in expanded intelligence, I had the modes of art, imagery, movement, and storytelling to enhance creativity. To do this, I added an expanded intelligence mode to each of the intelligences to use imagery. This system of instruction matched learning strengths for students from different cultures and with different learning preferences.

The intelligences were placed around a wheel starting in the metaphoric east since the sun rises in the east in the Northern Hemisphere where I live. Then the intelligences move around the learning wheel in a clockwise fashion, as Earth appears to rotate in the

Northern Hemisphere, my home. Practical intelligence focuses on facts and vocabulary. Technical intelligence is about problem solving, and conceptual intelligence is what Western learning theory calls higher-order thinking skills and includes storytelling. The north is creative intelligence used in projects.

The intent of writing and creating *The Learning Wheel* was to apply what I had learned from working with American Indian tribal education leaders and American Indian students, as well as from my doctoral training in learning theory and my imagery research. I saw human development along a continuum from emotional health to learning wisdom. If Carl Rogers and the other humanists were right—that humans have a creative force that, once contacted, could lead a person to health and healing—this could help people learn, maybe even in an accelerated manner. It was part of my journey to wisdom to see how to use the wheel and imagery for successful learning environments.

When one attends to each direction on the wheel, there is balance, and one gains synergy. The wheel can spin freely; to know and to love are the same. The idea of wheels and the goal of human development is balance and harmony. This helped me understand how storytelling could transform consciousness. Synergy is created when all four elements around the wheel are addressed.

Stories for Balance and Harmony

Wheels are the way to organize information and create endeavors that align with the creative energies of the earth. Wheels are circular in nature, and stories are a way of aligning with the cyclic nature of the earth, and also create balance and harmony. Stories work in a circular fashion, as in the metaphor of the hoop. Every story has an introduction followed by an event or conflict that is then followed by some sort of resolution, which is also a return to the beginning, or the place and time for the next story to start. In this circular fashion, stories mimic cycles on Earth (seasons), with the moon, and in the cosmos, as well as in human life.

Gregory Cajete is a Tewa from Santa Clara Pueblo, New Mexico, and a professor of Native American Studies. He is internationally recognized as an expert in using the indigenous wisdom of the "nature of nature." In indigenous societies, all creation originates from some form of myth that directly correlates to the natural environment surrounding them. This central myth places nature at the center of existence; therefore, all subsequent stories are nature-based. Most creation stories refer to a point of origin, or center, where life emerged.

Believing people are one with nature enables them to become keen observers and quickly recognize cyclical patterns. The seasons, availability of game, gathering plants, sprouting seeds, the lunar and sun cycles, and the menstrual cycle were constant reminders of Earth's cyclical patterns. These patterns led indigenous people to visualize circles and hoops in describing or artistically expressing these patterns. This overlapping and connected image, or concept of circles and hoops, is a template for relationships, myths, and stories.

Indigenous stories most often examine the complex mythological relationships between animal deities, humans, and the environment. It is understood that all events affect the future and therefore have deeper meaning, giving stories access to multiple realities. It is also understood that every action has ramifications that are both positive and negative. Inside the indigenous view of interconnectedness is the concept of reciprocity. Cajete explains that there is an instinctual understanding that to take life from these groups of animals, one must give back as well.

Most indigenous storytelling is spiritual and ultimately transformational. The hope and intent for many indigenous cultures was simply to live "the way" or "the path" in as happy and successful a way as possible. Contrary to today's view of all education as career training, indigenous societies recognized people's innate gifts and nurtured them toward a place and time when they could contribute more effectively to the group. Education was considered a community process. Using storytelling as it was initially developed in indigenous societies can return community awareness and a spiritual view of connectedness to nature back to education in a holistic manner.

By telling cultural stories or by creating their own stories, people can find their hidden strengths. Jung suggested the shadow in the unconscious as a mechanism for the conscious mind to hide trauma or other difficult memories for stability. He also proposed that there was a golden shadow—positive characteristics—that can strengthen a person. Telling and listening to stories is a way to tap into what's hidden in the golden shadow. Not only do stories heal, but they also contain wisdom.

With oral storytelling, humans enter a liminal realm connected to the collective unconscious where, over time, human wisdom resides. "Liminal" is derived from the Latin word *limen*, meaning a threshold, a transitional space. Shamans and priests of all religions use ceremonies to create such spaces. Michael Harner documents the ways shamans create liminal spaces with incense, candles, music, or drumming. Liminal spaces create an opening to a timeless dimension of interconnection. Storytelling creates these liminal spaces not only through the rhythm in the telling but also through the evoked emotions and images. When people hear a good story, their faces relax, and their eyes widen. Their minds are relaxed and open to deep wisdom. This happens, in part, due to the imagistic, circular, and emotional nature of story. Liminal and the limbic system (my favorite brain structure) stand for the edge or threshold from one state of consciousness to another. Even though there is no incense or drumming, there is a certain rhythm as people tell stories.

Storytelling is an oral account, which sets it apart from literate traditions of learning and knowledge. Storytelling can be a folktale, a performance by a professional storyteller, a cultural story by an elder, a telling of the day's events around the dinner table, a sharing at an AA meeting, an encounter that happened during childhood, or an insight from an ancestor's life. All humans are natural storytellers, as evidenced by the presence of storytelling in all cultures around the planet. Stories have been used by all societies since ancient times to teach cultural bonding and spiritual interconnectedness.

Storytelling is also the traditional method in societies for transmitting values and establishing cultural identity and self-concept. The light that all people are born with is strengthened with the wisdom that has been passed down from person to person in stories. This wisdom includes heroes and heroines, great feats, the spirit of perseverance, the character traits of discipline and courage, the ability to laugh at failures, the willingness to accept help when it is offered, and the refusal to give up hope. Stories portray human fears and adversities in vivid terms. They do not deny, avoid, or flinch from the tests in life. In fact, tests are often the core of the most potent stories. By providing maps of facing adversity, stories can heal the pain from abandonment, violence, racism, alienation, blocked opportunities, and negative expectations. Stories give humans a vehicle to express brother pain and then transform it with the archetypes and symbols of strength embodied by the main characters.

Stories' Purposes

Stories are valuable for many purposes.

- Learning respect for humans and nature
- Finding the interconnectedness of people
- Witnessing the continuity of life from the past, present, and future, which includes hope
- Understanding adversity is a natural form of life
- Achieving harmony and balance with nature
- Facing pitfalls with humor
- Discovering ways of staying safe
- Learning culture or family identification
- Acquiring positive character traits, particularly bravery
- Accessing maps of how to face and navigate adversity
- Observing one's place in life

From these purposes, it is clear that storytelling can assist people in finding psychological stability in their lives within the scope of the human experience. Stories tell humans where they came from and where they are going. Understanding the stages in stories shows how stories work to give listeners emotional resiliency. With emotional resilience, humans have a strong sense of self, such that the pitfalls and adversity of life do not overwhelm them. This leads to psychological growth since their psychic energy is not bound up in defending the ego. With a strengthened ego, the mind is cleared of reactive patterns.

Brother Blue was at the WHEEL Council's 1995 Storytelling for Prevention conference held in Tucson, Arizona. Tucson in February is magical. The courtyard of the conference hotel set the stage with fragrant orange blossoms. Brother Blue was dressed in blue brocade and a blue beret. I recall he might have had a staff adorned with blue scarves. He was magnetic. Adults and children surrounded Brother Blue, including my children, listening to his rhyming oral eloquence. This was one of the highlights of our non-profit's life, whose mission was to prevent drug and alcohol use and other destructive behaviors in young people by combining storytelling, the arts, and cultural empowerment with scientific research. One of my favorite quotes from Brother Blue is "Tell the story all time, so that every grain of sand and every work that ever will be, will hear it."

In 1995, I had received a grant from the Arizona Community Council to create Storytelling for Empowerment, a program for the Tohono O'odham Nation in Southern Arizona. I had been successful with the BA program in getting teaching credentials for tribal members, and at that time, I wanted to return to child development. I had been working on B. A. programs for working adults at Prescott College since 1980. Working with local tribal members and teachers, we created three curriculum books for middle school social studies, language arts, and physical education courses. At that time, there was available grant money for substance abuse prevention due to Nancy Reagan's pet project. I was ready to use this misguided simplicity to develop storytelling programs for fostering emotional strength. Of course, with my work in U.S. urban centers, tribal communities, and India, I was extremely interested in working in American Indian communities since they were underserved.

With what I had learned about storytelling, I loved what my friend Bernard Siqueros, Director of Education for the Tohono O'odham Tribe, told me: "You think wisdom comes from books, but we know it comes from our elders." I created a program to strengthen young people with stories and wrote grants for the WHEEL Council. I was able to get major foundation and federal grants from 1995 to 2008 and used them to develop the Storytelling for Empowerment program. We served hundreds of young people and thousands of families. We achieved evidence-based results of decreasing marijuana use due to an increasing perception of its harm, helping families work toward better health.

We created two curricula through the work of the WHEEL Council, receiving over three million dollars in grants over thirteen years. A stream of my career has been focused on empowering children, particularly those from diverse backgrounds. This was the period of my wisdom journey when I explored applications of imagery and storytelling. Initially, the Council worked on the Tohono O'odham Nation, and then we moved to downtown Phoenix, serving Mexican American youth.

The Storytelling PowerBook

I wrote the *Storytelling PowerBook* in 1997 to empower youth and prevent substance abuse. I followed up on this by writing the *HIV StoryBook* in 2003, aimed at preventing HIV infection. Many people have a misconception of prevention—that it is a one-shot deal, that a lecture here or there will solve the problem. I experienced an example of this when I was on sabbatical in Europe in 2007, visiting U.N. programs on substance abuse and HIV prevention. The World Food Program (WFP) in Rome, for example, held a puppet show to teach safe sex practices as a truck distributed food to service areas in Africa. The results from the research we did through the WHEEL Council showed that five to ten hours were necessary to make a change. Prevention is not just about knowledge; it also includes behavior and attitudes.

My *Storytelling PowerBook* has six lessons: knowledge power, skill power, personal power, character power, culture power, and future power. Storytelling is threaded through the curriculum. In skill power, students are taught to use a delaying tactic and given a script to act out risky scenes involving drug use or unsafe sex. The students then act out their stories of delaying risky behaviors. The personal power section includes cultural stories of a range of locations and cultures: Mexican, American, African American, Osage American

Indian, and Inuit. Many of the stories were written as plays so that the students could act them out.

The character power section uses historic U.S. figures, and their stories include Sequoyah, who invented a written language for his tribe, and Osceola, who fought against the Spanish invasion of what is now Florida. Thomas Paine is featured as well with his common-sense stories. The culture power section has students interview family members and friends to create their own stories of cultural identity and their bi- or multi-cultural identity. The future power section showcases stories of contemporary role models and prompts students to set future goals and write their future stories.

Young adult teacher aides led club sessions with this curriculum. We implemented it for many years. We published our findings in 2003 in an article, "Storytelling for Empowerment: Decreasing At-Risk Youth's Alcohol and Marijuana Use," in *The Journal of Primary Prevention*. We reported statistically significant decreases in marijuana use and increases in the perception of the harm of using drugs. A theoretical basis for the research was that stories could, by their very nature, be culturally affirming. We used cultural stories from around the world, plus the participants created stories from their own contemporary culture. Further, since the curriculum prompted them to tell their personal stories, they could express emotions in a safe manner through the art of storytelling.

There were 292 students who participated in the clubs and another 640 students who served as controls. Those participating went to a lot of club meetings, an average of 34 hours. We used a reliable assessment called the National Youth Survey. Club participants described their alcohol use as reduced to 0 times in the past 30 days and decreased marijuana use to under 1 time in the past 30 days, which is statistically significant. They also showed an increase in reporting that they could say no to alcohol when it was offered in comparison to the group that did not engage with the club materials. We were very pleased with the results, which showed that storytelling worked.

After this success, we received more federal funding to add HIV prevention to the substance abuse prevention effort, and the 2003 *HIV StoryBook* was developed to add to the club's activities, which

I wrote with two colleagues, Carolyn Orlando and Nola Murphy. This book was designed using *The Learning Wheel* model. Each major section—science, risk factors, relationships, and self-efficacy—used a turn around the wheel. For example, in the science section, there was a movement activity that taught facts about the human immunodeficiency virus (HIV), how it is transmitted, and how to prevent it. Students role-played scenes to show they knew the risks and acted out an English story, *John the True*. As in HIV transmission, blood plays a strong theme in this story, since the dragon's blood saved John the True. It seemed fitting, since HIV can be spread through blood.

The other lessons continue in a similar vein, with role-playing and cultural stories written so that they can be acted out in parts. The story for risk factors was *The Dragon's Robe*, where a young, orphaned Chinese woman who was a weaver keeps weaving despite many hardships. She personifies the character strengths of patience and perseverance. The point of the story is that sometimes it might be good to wait to engage in sexual activity. Our curriculum was based on solid learning theory, prompting students to practice buying and using condoms. The book culminates with participants creating their own stories. I used the storytelling cycle I adapted from Joseph Campbell's work. Participants were asked to write their own stories based on a test they had experienced in their lives, using the cycle to move their experience to the mythic realm.

Creating a Story

Here are the prompts for the story creation assignment.

- Choose an archetype to represent you in your story from a suggested list.
- Choose a name for the archetype.
- Choose a color that represents the archetype. This is done to activate the emotional center of the brain, the amygdala in the limbic system, and open memories to vivify the storytelling experience.
- Describe the test that the character experiences.

- Describe the helpers to get through the test. Helpers can be personal characteristics of the main character, people in the character's life, deities, mythic creatures, or even those who have passed. The key to using story for emotional strength and problem-solving skills is that there are always helpers to aid the main character in navigating tests. There will always be helpers for difficulties.
- Tell a story starting with a scene that is vivid in sensory detail and includes an ending.

Excerpt from *HIV StoryBook*

You can circle more than one.

BEGINNING YOUR STORY

Choose an Archetype from the list on the right for the main character.

Archetype of main character (see list at right): ________________________

____

Name of main character for the story: ________________________

Color associated with character: ________________________

Characteristics that are clear about the character (see list at right): ________________________

____

Characteristics that the character might need but that might be hidden or might seem negative. For example sometimes one needs to be vulnerable, or to take care of oneself and sometimes one needs to be angry. (See list at right):

____

____

MY TEST

____

____

MY HELPERS

____

Example of Archetypes

hero	warrior
priest	priestess
princess	wizard
monster	learner
prince	king
queen	scholar
artist	musician
painter	writer
movie star	beauty
handsome	mother
father	teacher
fool	rebel
magician	child
elder	wise person

Example of Characteristics

brave	strong
inquisitive	wise
curious	vulnerable
deep	insecure
wounded	loving
caring	creative
musical	afraid
ugly	angry
open	wondering
knowledgeable	foolish
innocent	trusting

My colleagues and I published an article in 2016 in *Journal of Adolescent Research* titled "Storytelling for Empowerment for Latino Teens: Increasing HIV Prevention Knowledge and Attitudes." We found that *HIV StoryBook* worked just as *Storytelling Power-Book* had worked. Our project was needed since HIV infection was higher for Latino adolescents than for their White counterparts. The theoretical basis for our program was Urie Bronfenbrenner's ecodevelopment theory. He was a famous psychologist who helped establish Head Start. According to Bronfenbrenner, if one wanted to create an effective youth development program, one needed to include the following systems: macrosystems (culture and social norms), exosystems (parents), mesosystems (peers), and microsystems (individual). We designed our storytelling program to address all these levels. Storytelling was a perfect fit because, as noted by Joseph Campbell, stories give humans context about where they came from and where they were going. In addition, family culture is transmitted with stories, and people find personal meaning in stories by identifying with characters' personality strengths and their ways of solving life's problems.

Our research reported quantitative and qualitative data. For the quantitative portion of the study, 50 Mexican American youths participated in the *HIV StoryBook* curriculum, and 46 from the same population participated in activities from a substance abuse prevention curriculum without HIV prevention content. We used an HIV prevention survey for pre- and post-measurement, which included the following: an efficacy of stopping sexual advances index, the ability to discuss sexual topics scale, and HIV prevention knowledge. We found that participants who had participated in club activities using *HIV StoryBook* were able to discuss sexual topics and reported an intention to stop sexual advances. They also had more HIV prevention knowledge. They also had more favorable attitudes towards condom use. This data was all good news. Our storytelling approach was working in prompting teens to be thoughtful about their sexual activity and to make good choices for their health.

Besides doing quantitative surveys with participants, we hired an anthropologist and her bilingual research assistant to do bilingual focus-group interviews with the participants and their mothers. In qualitative research, interviews are transcribed, and the researcher analyzes the transcripts for emerging patterns. We were excited about the results of this research. One of the biggest of these was what our anthropologist called "embodied curriculum," meaning participants reported using what they learned from the club in their day-to-day interactions with others. Another exciting theme was that participants reported improved family communication. This showed us that we were actually accomplishing what the Bronfenbrenner systems theory proposed—that we were affecting the family system with storytelling. Parents reported that their children were raising questions about what was happening with other family members who might be abusing substances or engaging in other risky behavior. Our storytelling approach was working.

Later, I used the same storytelling approach when I was asked to do an evaluation of youth development programs in Santa Barbara and Ventura County, California. The McCune Foundation had funded these programs to help youth to become active citizens. Sarah McCune was the publisher of Sage Publications, a famous publisher of research. We were enthusiastic to apply a storytelling approach to open the black box of these programs that helped low-income teens, many of whom were children of migrant workers employed in the vineyards. The results from our efforts, "Storytelling Narratives: Social Bonding as a Key to Youth at Risk," were published in the *Child & Youth Care Forum*.

I had learned from the teachings of American Indian culture that sometimes children and teens would disclose more if a third person was used. A facilitator who worked with the project led the participants in a group-storytelling track, and we designed a protocol where the participants told a story about a mythic person who experienced the program alongside them. We adapted the storytelling activity in *HIV StoryBook* to prompt groups of teens and pre-teens to tell the story about an imaginary character who, like them, had experienced the program. We used the following prompts. The reader will notice the similarity with the storytelling task from *HIV StoryBook*.

Another Way to Create a Story

Here are the prompts for writing about the mythic person or character who had experienced the program.

- Name of the main character
- Type of character (examples: hero, priest, princess, monster, prince, queen, artist, painter, movie star, handsome

     being, father, fool, magician, elder, warrior, priestess, wizard, learner, king, scholar, musician, writer, beauty, mother, teacher, rebel, child, wise person, or make up your own)
- Color associated with the character
- Age of the character
- Gender of the character
- Ethnicity, culture, or race of the character
- Language spoken at home
- Characteristics of the character (examples: brave, inquisitive, curious, deeply wounded, caring, musical, ugly, open, knowledgeable, innocent, strong, wise, vulnerable, insecure, loving, creative, afraid, angry, wondering, foolish, trusting, or make up your own)
- What was character like before ___________ (name of program)? At school? At home?
- What was difficult for the character in the ___________ (name of program)?
- What has helped with the difficulty? (This could be other people or something inside the character.)
- What is the character like now? At school? At home?
- How does the character affect the community around him or her?
- What is the end of the story?

Participants enjoyed the task, and the stories were quite telling. In all cases, the type of the main character was either a loner or a rebel, showing that the participants felt outside of the main social network in their schools. The tests that the main character experienced included bullying, not fitting in, and not knowing how to connect with others. There were two things that stood out from the stories: (1) the programs created a family-type atmosphere, where the participants felt accepted, and (2) the programs actually taught skills, such as how to work with computers, for example. It was inspiring to see how the participants saw the return of their imaginary colleague. The main character found a cure for AIDS, went to college, or gave his or her parents money. There was altruism in the participants' goals. Again, we were invigorated by the use of story, in this case, as a research tool to discover the effectiveness of youth development programs.

Our research results were very positive, and they supported what other researchers around the world had found out about using storytelling to increase young people's health. My research found that our storytelling was effective in decreasing Latino teenagers' alcohol and marijuana use from once per month to zero per month. Further, HIV prevention knowledge and attitudes increased. African psychologists, D. H. Balmer and others, have documented storytelling to increase safe sex skills. They worked with thirteen- and fourteen-year-olds in Nairobi, Kenya, using a storytelling and role-play approach about safe sexual behavior. They documented increases in a sexual self-efficacy scale (for example, refusing advances and using safe-sex practices). Several narrative-oriented HIV prevention programs report that story allows teens to clarify their personal values to make decisions about potentially self-destructive behaviors. This research shows that storytelling is a practical tool for helping young people learn values, spiritual strength, and skills to protect their health and thrive as they grow into adults.

Chapter Four: Storytelling Archetypes

Story Characters and Archetypes

As stories teach ancient human wisdom, the characters in stories show people how to transform. The main characters in stories are archetypes. Archetypes in ancient myths have literally transformed physically on their quest for wisdom, growing wings or losing their heads. I review deity transformational archetypes in my book *Archetypal Imagery.* I talk about Lilith, the Middle Eastern goddess and Adam's first wife, who grew wings as she fell from heaven because she had questioned God. Another is Isis, the great Egyptian Empress, who gained power by tricking the sun god Re to give her his name. Later, she had to grow wings to fly over the Nile in search of the body of her dead husband, Osiris. She mated with him to give birth to the extraordinary Pharaoh Horus.

A third deity was Avalokiteśvara, the Buddha of compassion. He had taken the *bodhisattva* vow to save all beings before he journeyed to Nirvana. However, he was so overwhelmed by the enormity of human suffering that his head shattered into hundreds of pieces. He was transported to the Pure Land, and the Buddha gave him ten heads and one thousand arms to do the work. The fourth deity that represented transformation to me was Ganesha, the Hindu elephant god. He was protecting his mom, Parvati, from his dad, Shiva, while she was taking a bath. Shiva is the Hindu god of destruction. His father did not take kindly to this and ripped off Ganesha's head, and then he replaced it with one from an elephant to stem Parvati's pleading.

These archetypes were given new heads and sprouted wings to transform into wisdom, a physical metaphor for the transformation. Letting go is a basic dictum of transformation, just as Cinderlad let go to face the munching monster. He was ready, but he had to let go of the outcome. The archetypes in these stories obviously met great crises that prompted their transformation. A great lesson from story is to face trauma and to find inner characteristics buried in the unconscious to solve life dilemmas. These archetypes from cultural stories teach the path to wisdom of accepting the crises in life to align with the power of the human spirit.

Storytelling can help a person identify with an archetype, since listeners are intuitively drawn to certain characters in stories. People have their favorite characters in movies, books, and TV shows, or in family, religious, or cultural stories. Through storytelling, people can find an archetype with whom they feel an intuitive connection. According to Jung, children unconsciously align with an archetype to organize their personalities. An archetype is a basic blueprint of the personality in the energetic domain—that liminal dimension without time and space orientation.

Humans live "in front of archetypes," which is to say, archetypes propel and motivate us. In other words, humans are trying to match a given energy pattern that will help propel development. This is an unconscious process for children, but it can be turned into a conscious one. Jung says, "You run your unconscious, or it will run you." By listening to stories, a person may "find" an archetype in a conscious manner that helps open the unconscious. "Finding" an archetype can be a natural process. Often, a person can develop a strong fascination with an archetype that is almost an itch that needs to be scratched that doesn't go away.

By identifying with an archetype, the conscious mind can focus on its energy pattern to open the unconscious mind. This clears an opening to receive insight. Ways of working with archetypes can be finding stories, visualizing the archetype in the mind, finding emotions that the archetype evokes in the body to sense and release, drawing the archetype, or moving the archetype. Possibly the simplest way to work with an archetype is to find a picture and a story about the archetype. Archetypal identification can open the mind by clearing a channel between the conscious and unconscious minds so that limited frames in the conscious mind that impede intuitive insight are softened.

Storytelling & Archetypal Identification

Archetypal identification can transform consciousness by creating a safe conduit from conscious awareness to the personal and collective unconsciousness. As a result, emotional reactive patterns are released, and spiritual insight can pop into awareness. In essence, archetypal identification can help people with emotional and spiritual development. Listening to stories, reading stories, or creating stories is a natural way to find an archetype for identification. People are drawn to and attracted to certain characters in stories. Identification is immediate. Finding an archetype is an intuitive exploration and a natural process. The ego keeps people out of the unconscious mind for stability, so it is not apt to open to the unconscious. However, storytelling relaxes the ego and opens the mind. It's not difficult; people are attracted to archetypes like magnets.

Archetypes and Individuation

As mentioned in Chapter One, an archetype is an energy pattern in the collective unconscious that conveys a given characteristic. For example, if someone sees an image of Hercules, that person may think of strength. If someone sees an image of Mother Theresa, a person might think of unconditional love or service. Children unconsciously and naturally align with one to give them stability and a sense of safety: they believe "This is who I am." If one observes a preschool playground, one can see the archetypes active as the children play: a hero, a helper, a teacher, a monster-bully, a beauty, or a strong man.

When a person experiences an archetype, they may sense different characteristics. However, there is usually one characteristic that stands out for a person. Archetypes speak to people differently, but they are all a lens to the collective unconscious, where human patterns of wisdom reside. The collective unconscious holds the patterns laid down by humans for solving life's dilemmas. They are the heroes and heroines whose tests, struggles, and feats model characteristics that, when embodied by listeners, can lead them to wisdom. Archetypal identification is the channel. It can lead to a state of individuation, which is the goal of development in Jungian psychology. This is a state where a person can act with freedom, as opposed to reacting to patterns buried in the unconscious. The mind is spacious, and information freely flows from the personal and collective unconscious. The mind is not reactive to emotional material in the unconscious. A spacious mind equates to inner wisdom or individuation.

Archetypal Identification: The Ego and the Self

In his book *Ego and Archetypes*, Edward Edinger, a famous psychiatrist and Jungian analyst, explains how archetypes act to move a person to individuation and wisdom. In Jungian psychology, the ego suppresses uncomfortable, difficult emotions and memories to create stability. But over time, the ego gets out of control, and more and more things are suppressed, limiting the psyche space a person has. In individuation, the topography of the mind has changed to allow spiritual insights to emerge from the unconscious, to allow rational thought to flow, and emotions to be felt and released. The mind has become soft, warm, open, and agile. An idea that is attributed to Jung is that either the unconscious runs you or you run your unconscious. If a person opens up awareness to the unconscious reactive patterns, prompted by unconscious material can be released. One can run the unconscious.

Edinger explains how this works. The Self is the whole of the inner being, which includes the ego and the unconscious. To be emotionally healthy, a person needs a secure sense of self. "Here I am, this is the space I inhabit, here are my boundaries, and here is where I start and end." The ego is functional and helpful. But over time, as mentioned above, it can get out of control and shove a lot of emotional material into the personal unconscious, which can impact stability. The ego essentially separates consciousness from the Self. However, as a person builds a secure sense of self, the ego relaxes and allows connection to the Self. Edinger calls this the ego-Self axis. This is emotional health. Information can move up through the axis for awareness. The person is moving towards wholeness, but there is still not a completely open channel.

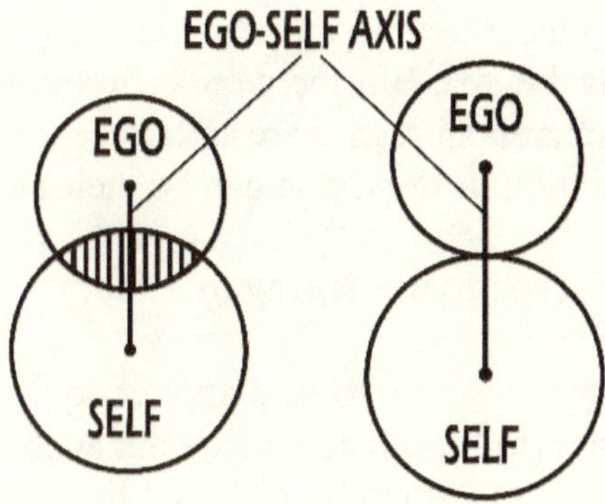

The next phase in development is called "individuation," which I consider wisdom. Edinger says when this happens, there is an animating loop where there is a free flow of information between the ego and the Self. A person is aware. A person is not reactive to triggers that awaken emotional material in the unconscious. A person has mental space to see family and societal stereotypes and expectations, but has the awareness to make choices about how to be with them. With individuation, a person can act in the world and not react. The person has freedom.

An archetype has the capacity to facilitate development towards individuation for both emotional health and spiritual insight, since spiritual insight from the collective unconscious can shine through to awareness. There is space in the mind, and awareness is keen.

Archetypes Create the Animating Loop Between Ego and Self

As mentioned above, an archetype is an energy pattern in the collective unconscious that conveys a way of being that can be embodied. As children align with an archetype to organize their personality, they are not necessarily consciously in touch with which archetype they are living in front of. But as a person's awareness increases, they become more aware of who they are. They are aware of the unconscious forces affecting their being. A person may consciously find out which archetype is motivating them. Identification with an archetype opens up a conduit to the unconscious in a safe manner. An archetype is like a facet of a prism that allows energy to move in and out.

Usually, in Jungian therapy, a person may connect with an archetype through their dreams. But the wonderful thing about storytelling is that the characters in stories are archetypes. When people connect with a character in a story, that can be their archetype.

Finding an Archetype by Listening to a Story

People often wonder how to find an archetype. But it is simple in the world of storytelling. It is a character with whom one has a connection. There is an attraction, a "Yes, I like this character."

When I was young, my mother would read me stories. One was from the book *Told Under the Green Umbrella*. It was the story of Cinderlad. I will relate this story frequently in this book, but the important part here is my identification with one of the characters as an archetype. Cinderlad must go through many hardships. For example, he is bullied by his brothers and faces a monster that eats his family's fields each year. But his hardships are rewarded. Each year when he faces the monster, he gets a horse and gilded bridles and saddles. Over three years, he got bronze, silver, and gold sets. At the same time, the King wants to find a consort for his Princess. He puts the Princess atop a glass hill with three apples in her lap. The knight who can ride to the top of the hill and get the apples will win her hand. All the other knights fail, but Cinderlad, on subsequent days, using the different sets of bridles and saddles, rides up and gets the apples. When hearing this story, some people might focus on Cinderlad. But for me, as a young child, I was attracted to the Princess on the Glass Hill. One could wonder what the attraction was, but for me, it was about aspiration, to be on the glass hill that others would see as being valued. I think the Princess was my archetype.

Archetypes Can Change

The archetype that one identifies with can change. I remember my hippie-new age era when people were making shamanic journeys to find their power animal. People would say, "I found a bear. A bear is my power animal." Or, people would say, "I saw a leopard. My power animal is a leopard." Power animals are archetypes; they are an energy pattern that conveys a given characteristic. A bear could usually convey strength, for example; a leopard could convey cunning. People thought they would always have the same power animal. However, Maria-Louise von Franz, a Jungian therapist and colleague of Jung, said that every archetype contains every other archetype. Archetypes can change. The quartz has many facets, which are different archetypes. Any facet allows access to the center, opening access to the unconscious. Because of this, it doesn't matter which archetype a person finds, and archetypes can change and transform over time.

Finding an Archetype, Creating a Story

A story I made up showed me how to find an archetype by creating one's own story. I was doing workshops to teach professionals how to use imagery. At that time, in the late 1990s, the area of psychoneuroimmunology was popular. Candice Pert's research on neurotransmitters showed that these transmitters could communicate with immune cells. Previously, it was thought that the neurological and immune systems were totally separate. But with new research, it was clear that the two systems could talk, i.e. brain transmitters talking to immune cells. Neurotransmitters are released when people experience emotions. Thoughts that evoke emotions activate neurotransmitters. This meant that thoughts could affect immune functioning. Psychologists like Jeanne Achterberg documented that thinking in pictures or the cognitive process of imagery could engender emotions. Achterberg, working with cancer patients, found she could help patients image T cells, and this would increase their attack on cancer cells.

I was giving a workshop for nurses and wanted to help nurses realize that the unconscious was a friendly place and could activate healing. I'd been working with storytelling for health for many years and thought stories would be a good way to get this point across. I wanted a character who symbolized the healing nature of the unconscious. I thought of a dragon as this symbol. With my allegiance to being a vegetarian, I made the dragon a vegetarian, and the protagonist was a young woman who was multi-racial. Her race was determined by the time of day. Her village was like a time long ago and a time far in the future. Everyone in the village was afraid of the dragon since they thought he had wiped out a village. The village had created a tradition of sacrificing the most successful young lady every ten years.

I named the young woman Sophia. The name just came to me. In my story, Sophia changed the tradition of sacrificing young women. She allowed the village to take her to the sacrificial point, but she changed the rules by making friends with the vegetarian dragon, Claude, and stopping the sacrificial cycle. The story was surprisingly popular. I thought, "Who is Sophia?" A whole journey with Sophia ensued in my life, with Sophia becoming my archetype. I found out she was a Middle Eastern goddess and possibly Jehovah's mother. She was the creator in the Dead Sea Scrolls. As a creator, she did not look down from above; she created the material world out of her own spirit. Her name was derived from the Greek word *sophos*, translated as wisdom. In a book on the history of philosophy, the book title has her name, *Sophie's World.*

Since the story was popular, and since my initial research into her name revealed amazing facts, I thought that Sophia was an archetype I should be working with. It seemed she was everywhere I looked. I would walk into a bookstore, pick up a book, and there would be Sophia. I found the book *Sophie's World* by Jostein Gaarder. Then I found a feminist Christian scholar, Susan Cady, who wrote a lot about Sophia. I studied all these sources to create a picture of Sophia, to figure out what drew me to her, or why I found her. Sophia was iconoclastic, a strong presence that questioned the patriarchal view of creation. Sophia was about interconnection, spirit in matter, not spirit over matter. A part of Sophia was ineffable, almost a mystery. But the characteristic I settled on was interconnection.

Buffalo Woman: Archetype of Commitment

Different people reading stories or hearing stories will be attracted to different characters, but one of the characters may become a person's archetype. In the story *Buffalo Woman,* a man falls in love with a woman who is not from his tribe. They have a child together. But his tribe rejects her, bullying her and treating her with disdain. She leaves her tribe and goes back to her own tribe of Buffalo people. She transforms into a buffalo, and her son does as well. The husband is committed to his wife and son and follows them. Over time, he passes the test of finding his wife and son, even though they are buffalo. The herd of buffalo wants the husband to find his son amongst the herd. His son gave him a clue that he would flip his tail, and the husband passed the test. The husband is then initiated into the buffalo tribe, as other buffalo submit him to a test of rolling over him repeatedly. He then becomes a buffalo and can be with his wife and son. If one is attracted to this character, the husband of the Buffalo Woman, then one may find a characteristic that attracts. The husband has many characteristics. It could be loyalty; it could be devotion; it could be love; it could be bravery. It is up to the listener to connect and to decide. The connection to an archetype is intuitive. It is not a cognitive decision that one likes the characteristic. It is an attraction, possibly somatic, and the characteristic will reveal itself.

The White Spider: Archetype of Unconditional Love

Other listeners may find an archetype in the story *The White Spider*. In this story, a young man, Piki, meets a woman who happens to dock her canoe by his house. He falls in love with her, and she loves him. It turns out over time that she is the chieftain's daughter, preventing them from marrying. Soon, the chieftain sets up a competition. The man who brings the most beautiful gift will win his daughter's hand. Piki gives up because he is poor, even though he still loves the chieftain's daughter. However, the White Spider weaves a beautiful shawl for him to give to the chieftain's daughter. At the end of the story, Piki wins her hand because of the beautiful shawl. The White Spider created the shawl for Piki because she knew of Piki's humility and devotion. A reader might be drawn to Piki for one of his characteristics.

The Children: Archetype of Self-Respect

The Children has a strong archetype of a wise, elder woman. A community holds the elderly woman in respect. The village has had difficulty birthing children, and they go to the elder for herbs. She gives them the right herbs, and the people of the community start having babies, even twins. For a while, the community showed their respect to the elder, harvesting her crops and doing maintenance on her house. But over time, they forgot about her. Then a disease overtook the village, and their children became sick. The community went back to the elder for help, but she said to them, "You've forgotten me." The community members had to make amends and start helping the elder again. She stood up for herself, and as a result, she received respect. Self- respect created respect. A reader in a difficult situation may be attracted to the wise, elder woman. Identifying an archetype is not a thoughtful plan; it comes with an immediate attraction.

Isis: Archetype of Transformation

Other readers might want to foster bravery within themselves. Isis is a likely archetype to identify with for this characteristic. Isis is one of a set of quadruplets. Also, Isis is special since she tricked the sun god Re into telling her his name, giving her power. She and her sister and brothers have a complicated story. One of her brothers is Osiris whom she falls in love with and marries. Another of her brothers is Seth, who is jealous of all of them and eventually murders Osiris. Her sister Nephthys helps Isis find Osiris. After Isis finds Osiris' body on a sand bank, she mated with him and as a result, birthed Horus, who becomes a great Pharaoh. Isis can transform death into the creation of a great leader for Egypt. I've been attracted to Isis because she can take on huge challenges.

Xenophobe: Archetype of Strategy and Cunning

An archetype's job is to help people face the ups and downs in life to help them embody a characteristic that will help navigate these tests and transform. This process is sometimes called the hero-heroine journey, with the archetype being the hero or heroine. Often heroes need to use some cunning to navigate tests. Xenophobe, as a young dragon, needs to figure out how not to die. There had been an agreement between the dragons and the humans that a young dragon would come down out of the mountains and pretend to fight a human and then let the human kill him. In this way, the humans let the dragons live in peace. Xenophobe grew up in a storied manner high in the mountains, among lakes and granite slabs. But he grew up without a father, and he never understood what happened to his father. His mother was warm and loving, but there was a quality of sadness that carved lines on her face.

One day, his mother told him the agreement that dragons had made with the humans. A young dragon must die in a shilled fight. Xenophobe has been selected as a sacrifice. He goes along with it, but he had secretly created a plan. When the time comes, he comes down out of the mountain to meet the human by a lake. Instead of pretending to fight and then allowing the human to kill him, Xenophobe picks up the human and flies into the sky. They move beyond the stratosphere and grab a star to bring it back as a symbol of healing between humans and dragons. No longer does a dragon need to die as a meaningless symbol of peace. Archetypes can transform consciousness by creating a symbol that mobilizes new ways of being and knowing.

John the True: Archetype of Sacrifice

John the True is a complicated story. To simplify it and to feature John's characteristics as an archetype, this summary focuses on John's actions to save his King and the King's wife and their children. The King falls in love with a woman after seeing a painting of her. She lives in a warring kingdom, and John manages to bring her to the King. On the ship voyage, Ravens appear to John and make prophecies of how the King and Queen will be killed. The Ravens told John that he must not tell anyone, or John will be turned into stone. The prophecies come true, but John intervenes and prevents the King and Queen's demise. He must knock a cup of wine out of the King's hand; he must kill a dragon that is waiting. But eventually, John turns to stone. The Queen finds a way to bring him back to life. John is willing to sacrifice himself to protect the King and his family's lives. Hearing or reading the *John the True* story, a reader might be attracted to loyalty or bravery.

Keep on Steppin': Archetype of Patience

Jim was a slave and was abused. He has to work, day and night, and his master kept promising that he would free Jim. One day, the master's children are boating in a pond, and as the boat turns over the children almost drown. Jim swims out and saves them. Jim is thanked, but the master doesn't immediately free him, and tells him that if he works one more year, he will free him then. When that year is over, he says just one more year, Jim swallows his anger and betrayal and does the work. Finally, he is free. He gathers his meager belongings and walks off the property. The master and family call to Jim, "Haven't I been good to you? We all love you. You can't leave us." But Jim keeps on steppin'. Jim used his patience to finally be free. Jim has so many characteristics like industry, bravery, commitment, and more.

Finding an Archetype

One activity I often do is to help people find an archetype by thinking of their favorite story when they were young. I mention that it could be a story someone read, a TV show, a movie, or a tale told by a family member, for example. Then I ask the person to think about a character from that story. That often presents an archetype. In my book, *Archetypal Imagery and the Spiritual Self,* I have quizzes to find an archetype. One of my students took the quiz and found Ganesha, the Hindu elephant deity. She looked around her house with new eyes and found elephants throughout her house. A shower curtain, a statue, a vase. Sometimes our archetype is hiding in front of us.

Chapter Five: The Storytelling Cycle

"When the hero quest has been accomplished through the
penetration of the source, or through the grace of some male or
female, human or animal personification, the adventurer still
must return with his life-transmuting trophy."
-Joseph Campbell

Most stories use the hero/heroine stages documented by Joseph
Campbell in *The Hero with a Thousand Faces,* first published a year
after I was born in 1949. He had degrees in English literature and
medieval history, and he lived from 1904 to 1967. He studied French
and Sanskrit as a student in Paris and Munich. He employed a rig-
orous self-study program of five hours a day for five years. He was
a professor of literature at Sarah Lawrence College in comparative
mythology and religion. On a trip with his family to Europe, he discovered the philosophy of Krishnamurti, who, for a while, was a
guru for the Theosophical Society, a religion integrating concepts
from Hinduism and Buddhism. Later, Krishnamurti refused the
mantle of guru, and he became a spiritual teacher who challenged
people to find spirit within themselves. His work continues at the
Krishnamurti Education Center in Ojai, California. Campbell's time
with Krishnamurti seemed to influence his studies, as he focused on
themes expressed through the human spirit in myths from around
the planet, revealing common patterns, themes, and symbols that
supported Jung's idea of the collective unconscious.

Campbell proposed a cosmogenic round for understanding the
cycle of stories. It is a beautiful thing, since it depicts the nature of
stories that emerge from the unknown, the deep well of human wisdom in the collective unconscious. It reveals itself and then withdraws.
With poetic language, Campbell writes, "The sea of slumber…imagery

of myth awakes the flow of reality into the wakefulness from the unconscious dark and then dissolves into timelessness, repeating itself." As Campbell believed, "What could be a more vivid expression of transformation of consciousness than to be awakened?"

Campbell's Stages of the Hero's Journey

These are the stages I adapted from Campbell's book, *The Hero With a Thousand Faces*.

Normal Life: There is a steady state. Then a "call to adventure" happens that changes everything, if the character says yes.

Separation: The character must leave home or family to prove his character or to help others.

Tests: The character goes through very serious tests that prove his or her character. These initiations include battles, dismemberment, journeys into the unknown, and abduction. The character often has helpers during these tests.

Return: The hero or heroine returns after the initiation to his or her society, community, and family. By surviving the tests, the hero or heroine gives hope that others can survive. The hero or heroine brings back knowledge or a symbol or accomplishes a great feat that will help the community and family.

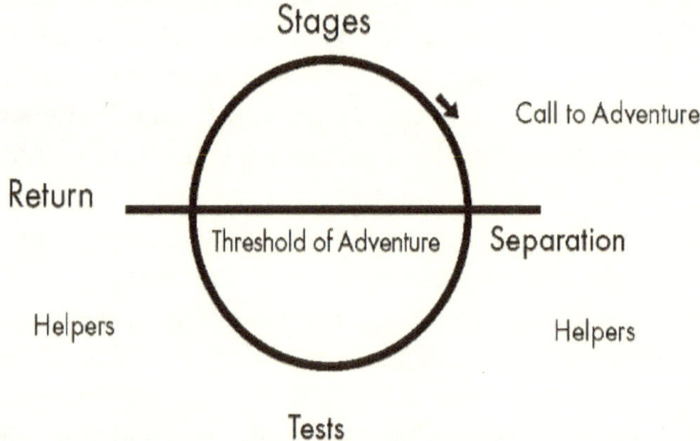

Examples of the Stages

Call to Adventure-Separation

Before the call to adventure, life starts in a normal manner for the main character. Then something happens that skews everything, and a different reality apart from what the main character knows as normal begins. Campbell says, "The passage of the magical threshold is a transit into a sphere of rebirth." The story of the Buddha is an apt example to illustrate these stages. Before becoming the Buddha, he was a pampered prince. However, there was a call to adventure in his story when he accidentally visits a place where the untouchables live, showing him for the first time the suffering in the world. The Buddha separates from his life as he knows it and goes off on a journey to find the meaning of life.

The separation stage in stories shows that life changes, sometimes in abrupt and painful ways. It also shows that people change and grow as a result of their interactions in life. In the call to adventure and separation, the character crosses the first threshold that metaphorically can be a desert, jungle, deep sea, or an alien land. The passage of the magical threshold is a transit into a sphere of rebirth.

One story I learned to tell was *John the True.* When one works with cultural stories, there is always the danger of cultural appropriation, of taking on stories or practices from other cultures as one's own. When I was a graduate student at the University of Kansas, I worked for a man named Don Bushell, who received millions of dollars in federal grants as part of Lyndon B. Johnson's Great Society. The program was called Follow Through. Head Start graduates made progress, but they didn't retain it when entering kindergarten. Dr. Bushell had a program called Behavior Analysis; it was designed to help kindergarten through third graders maintain and increase academic gains. In his model, there were three parent aides in each classroom, the curriculum was individualized, and students earned tokens to exchange for fun activities.

People think evidence-based results are a new concept in 2020, but back then, the U.S. Department of Health and Human Services had endorsed 19 models to see which had data showing they worked.

It was quite a job for me as a twenty-two-year-old. I'd travel to inner-city schools in Indianapolis, the Bronx, Philadelphia, the Northern Cheyenne Nation in Montana, and the Hopi Nation in Arizona to train these models. I thought I was doing a good job of hiding my hippie, vegetarian, yogi, adherent-to-natural-cures persona. I bought a designer suit and worked on my professional presentation. But one of the teachers called me her "hippie consultant." I smoked marijuana, but only on weekends. I was more interested in data than hippie sensibilities.

One of my colleagues took a job as a trainer for the Behavior Analysis model on the Hopi Nation and lived in the village of Moenkopi there. I visited frequently and noticed what was happening with hippies coming to the Hopi Nation to set up crystal circles and camp out in sacred places. The tribal members were appalled and furious at this appropriation. It was a good lesson for me to be careful. When I started the non-profit using storytelling for substance abuse and HIV prevention, I was mindful of this and would only use published stories or those that I was given permission to retell.

Prescott College's program was funded by the Arizona Humanities Council in 1990, and was called Native American Voices: Culture and Learning. I had been told by my mom I was Scottish, so I learned a way to tell stories at the conference. (Later, my daughter did a DNA test, and I had the data showing that I was 65 percent Scottish.) The story I learned was quite complicated, but it had a good demonstration of the first stage of the hero/heroine cycle, the call, and the return.

John the True

I return here again to *John the True*. There was a young King who had just inherited a kingdom. He had a devoted manservant, John the True. They were touring the castle and found some rooms in the basement with stored artwork. They came across a painting of a beautiful young woman. Her skin was as white as snow, her cheeks as red as blood, and her hair as black as ebony.

It is common in stories to use colors to make the scenes vivid. This fits with what research reports about effective imagery. When it is multisensory, the brain responds as if the scene is being perceived.

The King was smitten and spent days mooning over the beautiful woman. John could not console him, and he became committed to finding this young woman. It turned out that she was the Princess of the neighboring kingdom that had been at war over the young King's land for many years. John told the young King, "I will go and get her for you." He asked the King to get him a ship loaded with gold furniture.

Before this call to adventure, there was a normal state of affairs, which was the new King assuming his reign to take over the kingdom. In this story, a change occurred while the King was exploring his castle. That is when he discovered the picture of the beautiful woman. At the sight of the painting, everything changed—this is the call to adventure.

Tests

In the next stage of the storytelling cycle, the main character endures many tests. The Buddha's story exemplifies the fundamental, visceral nature of tests in stories: he nearly starved from fasting too much, people beset him in the wilderness, and his faith was severely tested. Tests in stories are no walk in the park. In some of the old cultural stories, there are brother battles, duels with dragons, or encounters with dangerous animals, like Jonah being swallowed by a whale. The severe tests in stories make it clear to the listener that adversity abounds in life. Listening to the tests characters face prompts listeners to accept life's traumas and provides a map for facing their own, offering hope that they will emerge, survive, and thrive.

Through stories, people can safely experience the trauma of life, as a story is a third-person account of events instead of the listener's actual life events. Stories of abusive parents, rape, abandonment, divorce, betrayal, disloyal friends, messages of inadequacy and ignorance, poverty, and societal oppression lose their sting when they are happening to a mythical character. However, listeners can use the story to extricate the demons of an individual life vicariously and see how characters map the healing and integration of such traumatic experiences. A third-person account removes feelings of shame and inadequacy, since people are talking about a character outside themselves. Also, many therapeutic programs use storytelling, as people tell stories of their lives.

Tests can be very significant. Being swallowed into the belly of a whale is metaphorically, in effect, is being swallowed into the unknown. It becomes a process of self-annihilation—losing the old self and forming a new self whose mettle has been proven by the tests. The main character undergoes a metamorphosis.

In *John the True*, there are many tests for many characters. Since the title has John's name, I'll focus on him. John has to figure out how to spirit the Princess away from her kingdom of the Golden Horde. He actually tricks her, luring her aboard to see the golden furniture, and then he sets sail while she is in the hold of the ship. The second test happens on the voyage back to the young King's land. As the Princess sits on the deck, three Ravens fly overhead, and their calls sound out a warning. John can understand animal language and is alarmed by three warnings. He can avert them, but if he tells why he is acting, he will turn to stone.

The Ravens say the Princess will be killed by a horse out of control, and the only way to save her is to cut off the horse's head. Second, at the wedding dinner, the King will drink poisoned wine, and someone must hit away the cup before he drinks it. Third, on their wedding night, a dragon will enter their bed chamber and slay them both. The Ravens caution John that if he warns them, then he will turn to stone. John must figure out how to face these tests without turning to stone.

Helpers

The best part of the storytelling cycle is the helpers' phase, since stories show that helpers naturally come to people during these tests. For example, the Buddha had the help of sages who told him to take the middle way, the path of moderation. He didn't need to fast; he just needed to find awareness. In European folktales, the enduring love of a dead parent is often the main helper, as in Cinderella's father, who inspires her to live her values even though she is abused. Also, magical figures can be helpers, as in a fairy godmother. Helpers can also be characteristics of the main character. For example, a characteristic that helps Cinderella is her work ethic, or one that helps the Buddha is his perseverance. Often, the tests bring out hidden characteristics, such as Jonah's belief in God even as a whale swallowed him.

Storytelling is an ancient human technology to transmit human wisdom from generation to generation. Stories teach ways of staying safe. Grimm's Fairy Tales taught children to stay out of the woods and not talk to strangers, using a big bad wolf. Stories also teach a context of human existence—where humans come from and where they are going. Elders of the Hopi tribe have an oral tradition detailing cosmology and how the material world came into being. The people emerged from the underworld.

Creation stories give humans a grounded foundation to feel connected to the earth, their family, and their tribe or community. Stories also showcase ways of facing adversity, surviving, and thriving. The great teaching of stories is that there is help for a person to endure tests, move through them, and go beyond to transform. The wisdom of stories is to showcase how to find helpers who can be:

- other people
- loved ones who have passed
- deities or supernatural help
- mythic figures or animals
- skills
- characteristics
- dreams and intuitions

In *John the True*, John has many helpers. First is a characteristic: John's loyalty to the King. He will do most things to help him. Second, John has problem-solving skills. He figures out how to trick the Princess away from her kingdom. Thirdly, John receives supernatural help from the Ravens, and he combines that with his skill of understanding animal language. Fourth, another characteristic—John is brave. As the story progresses, John stops all the dangers that have been predicted. He cuts off the horse's head, he dashes the cup of poison from his King's lips, and he hides in the bridal chamber and slays the dragon.

He keeps silent so that the King will not die, but finally the King is so puzzled by John's behavior that he demands an explanation. John must tell him, and as he does, he turns to stone. Later in the story, the Queen has a dream that helps her return John to life by using the dragon's blood that John had killed to save her life. The Queen becomes John's helper, but she has her own helpers: her dream and her belief in the truth of it.

Return

The final stage in the storytelling cycle is the return stage in which the main character has been transformed in some way and returns to a new normal. Joseph Campbell says, "For the mythological hero is the champion not of things become but of things becoming. The dragon to be slain by him is precisely the monster of the status quo." The main character crosses the return threshold usually with an internal transformation that is a gift back to the community, such as new insights, new characteristics, or enhanced strength. For example, the Buddha returned to society, but he was changed. He had brought back a gift to his community in his "new" being, transformed from spiritual insights that he could teach others. On Cinderella's return, she becomes a queen, supporting her king and her country with the new realization that she did not deserve abuse and that she was no longer a victim. For those who are not living the mythical proportions of the Buddha or Cinderella, this type of transformation can happen as well.

There is quite a dramatic return in *John the True.* John had become a stone statue, placed in the courtyard under the window of the wedding bed chamber. Time passes, and the King and Queen now have beautiful twin sons. The twins march in the courtyard, pretending to be soldiers, and salute John, as his story has been told and retold. The Queen has a dream in which she is told to scrape some of the blood off the floor from when the dragon was slain. Luckily, it is still there. The Queen is to put blood on the statue to revive

John. She does this, and it works. John is returned to life. This is common in stories—a rebirth, a return from death. There is a new normal which is sometimes a new life. In this case, the King and Queen are married with two sons, and John the True has returned, demonstrating that his sacrifice and loyalty acted as helpers. The return of the hero also brings a gift for the community, and in this case, John has brought a royal family to the Kingdom.

All humans experience tests in life, such as the death of a parent, financial crises, divorce, or difficulties at work. The hero/heroine stages help people navigate these adverse experiences by encouraging people to look for helpers. The storytelling cycle also foretells that there will be a return. People will come out of the test and be different from what they imagined, taking on a new role in their family or society.

Because of the strength of the stages of stories, listening to stories and beginning to learn to tell stories can actually impart emotional resiliency. Because stories are in the non-rational realm, the meaning, or moral, of a story need not be explained. The metaphors and symbols work at an unconscious level. The changes in the hero or heroine on return may be a felt sense, an energy shift. Campbell poetically typifies the fact that on the return, the main character is transformed and brings a gift to the community: "When the hero-quest has been accomplished, through the penetration of the source, or through the grace of some male or female, human or animal personification, the adventurer still must return with his life-transmuting trophy."

Resiliency in the Return

Stories teach resiliency in many ways:

- **A sense of inner strength.** Stories bond people with their geographic, cultural, and familial realities by giving values and "ways of being" that humans in the listener's situation have used for centuries. Through this, stories pass on cultural affiliation.

- **Future orientation.** Stories give a sense of continuity with the past and give patterns to use in the future.
- **Ability to laugh at oneself.** Story characters like Coyote and Br'er Rabbit often make fools of themselves but also win in the end, showing that mistakes are a normal part of life.
- Problem-solving skills. Attitudes, character traits, and even actions that help people face and thrive from adversity are showcased in stories.
- **Character traits.** Stories show that courage, love, kindness, vulnerability, weakness, strength, perseverance, fear, and anger are all part of the human condition and can serve to propel personal transformation and change. The characters in stories can also serve as role models to the listeners to inspire hope and motivation.

Cinderlad

The story *Cinderlad* depicts the storytelling cycle. This story is derived from the *The Princess on the Glass Hill*. I return to it again to give more detail. In this story, Cinderlad is the youngest of three brothers who live with their widowed father on a farm near Florence, Italy. In the story, his brothers terrifyingly bullied Cinderlad, hitting him and berating him. "You're so stupid, you're so dirty. No one cares about you. We all wish that you were never born." Cinderlad was forced to sit in a corner of the hearth when he wasn't toiling in the fields from dawn to dusk. Hence his name—he was always covered with ash cinders. Whenever their father bought Cinderlad clothes, the brothers stole them, and they also talked their father into ostracizing the boy as well.

One year on St. John the Baptist Day, near the summer solstice, the family went to sleep as usual. But they were awakened by a horrifying sound as if a giant was munching their wheat while the earth shook. (I was actually in Florence, Italy, on June 24, St. John the Baptist's Day. I was camping high above the city, and the fireworks rocked the ground. It was a truly beautiful and remarkable experience.) Come daylight, they found all their crops eaten down to stubs. Luckily, they had enough wheat to get them through the winter. On the next St. John the Baptist Day, the elder brother said, "I'll go sleep out in the hut in the fields and slay whatever monster it is." He had a swagger and arrogance, confident that he would succeed. Cinderlad volunteered, but the brothers said, "You're an imbecile. You cannot help." However, the elder brother spoke too soon. In the middle of the night, the earth shook again, and there was a horrendous munching sound. The family soon heard the brother banging on the door to be let in. In the morning, all the wheat was gone. Things were pretty grim, but the family still had some grain stores.

St. John the Baptist Day was approaching again, and again Cinderlad volunteered to help, and again his help was spurned. The second brother stuck out his chest, paraded around, and claimed, "I can do what no other man can do." But alas, the same thing occurred, and he was beating on the door to be let in after the earth started to shake.

Things were not going well for the family. It was the advent of the next St. John the Baptist Day after three years with no crops. The brothers and the father looked downtrodden, and Cinderlad came out of the hearth and said, "I'm not sure I can do it, but I will try." The family was desperate; he was given the go-ahead.

Cinderlad went out to the hut in the middle of the field and fell asleep. He was awakened by the earth shaking and a monstrous chomping sound. He went outside, shaking from fear, and said, "If it doesn't get much worse, I think I can stand it." The shaking started to abate, and then all was quiet. To his amazement, he saw a beautiful stallion standing there with a bronze set of armor. Cinderlad took the prize to hide in a corral by the river that no one knew about. The next morning, the wheat was waving in the wind on a bright, sunshining day.

Cinderlad returned home, but there was no praise. His brothers kept putting him down, saying it was just crazy luck. The same events happened the next two years on St. John the Baptist's Day, and Cinderlad stopped the destruction of his father's wheat. In the subsequent two years, things happened as in the first year. The earth shook, and a monstrous munching noise began. Each time, Cinderlad said, "If it doesn't get much worse, I think I can stand it." What changed each time was the type of suit of armor he was given. After the bronze suit, the next year it was silver, and then it was gold.

The family prospered, but Cinderlad's status did not change. However, things were soon to change. A call went out from the King to find a suitable husband for his daughter. He said that he would put her atop a glass hill with three golden apples in her lap, and the man who could ride up the hill and get the apples would be her husband and become the new King.

Princes and warriors came from far afield. But no one could get to the top of the glass hill. They would start far off, take a long run to gain momentum, and then charge up the hill. Some made progress but then slid back. Then one fine day, a knight on a great stallion with a bronze suit of armor came out of the woods. Riding up to the top of the hill, he took one apple. Onlookers cheered, but the knight rode back to the forest. The next day, the same thing happened, but this time the knight had on a silver suit of armor. On the third day, the knight had on a gold suit of armor. Each day after retrieving one of the apples, the knight disappeared into the forest.

The King put out a call for the mysterious knight to show himself. He sent messengers throughout the land to find him. The messenger came to Cinderlad's farm. As the messenger stood at the door, Cinderlad stood up from the hearth, but his brothers pushed him away. Cinderlad saw the information, though, and he went to the King's great hall where the Princess sat on a dais. The doors to the hall swung open, and Cinderlad came in clothed in sooty rags. People started yelling at him, "Get out of here!" But Cinderlad would not be deterred. He walked up to the Princess. He threw off his rags and stood there in golden armor. He said, "I have one apple. I have two apples. I have three." He put the golden apples in the Princess's lap. They were married, and they became kind and revered rulers.

Cinderlad had great resiliency. He was bullied and had few material comforts. He had a strong sense of self that overrode the external abuse. One thing that stands out in the story is that the brothers were arrogant, which masked their fear and insecurity. In contrast, Cinderlad was humble yet had confidence. His mantra kept him going: "If it doesn't get much worse, I think I can stand it." He had an openness in his attitude toward the world. He also had the magical help of the forces that would ruin his family's crop each year. When he stood up to them—actually bore witness to these forces—he was awarded great riches.

I used Cinderlad's mantra when I was on a bicycle tour in Quebec. It was a great trip led by Discovery Bicycles. They set up a series of routes each day. One could do a short loop or add an additional loop. I had done a bicycle trip the previous year in France, near Mount Ventoux in Provence, one of the routes for the Tour de France. Everyone else on the trip seemed to be triathletes. I was the slowest going up the hills and was sometimes shoved into the van since I was descending wrong or too slow. It wasn't too great for my self-esteem. But on this trip in Quebec, I seemed to be one of the fastest. On one of the last days, we were cycling through the town of Sutton, Quebec, and I chose to go the extra loop which had lots of staircase hill climbs amid the majestic display of maples in brilliant reds and oranges. I used Cinderlad's mantra up the hills: "If it doesn't get much worse, I think I can stand it." I had the best cycle of my life.

Stories help people find symbols for a strong self-identity and cultural affiliation. Hero and heroine endeavors showcase strategies of problem-solving skills and can become models for both youth and adults. Stories told by family members promote bonding and strength. Stories can help foster self-efficacy and teach resiliency.

After characters experience dire fates in stories, listeners see the traits that are necessary to withstand negative forces, succeed, and triumph. It is interesting to note that stories teach that most help from others comes from the heart of our favorite characters, as well as from the heart of the storyteller. Sometimes stories give spiritual strength. The hearer can gain the feeling of caring from the teller or the characters in the story. Love also helps our heroes and heroines succeed. This affective dimension of stories aids transformational learning and resiliency-building.

Metaphors and Symbols in Stories

Metaphors and symbols represent knowledge in a non-rational manner, which allows them to carry multiple meanings. Stories then contain emotional and spiritual content, unlike literal, linear knowledge content. Russel Thornton is Cherokee and a professor of anthropology at UCLA. He specializes in the population history of the peoples of the Americas. He compares indigenous creation stories to scientific explanations of origins. He states that there are two parallel knowledge systems from different paradigms that do not contradict each other, but each holds its own unique knowledge.

Similarly, Paula Allen Gunn is a member of the Laguna Pueblo, a literary critic, an activist, and a novelist. She was a professor at the University of New Mexico. She is known for questioning European scholars' view of women's roles in American Indian societies. She states the following: "Psychospiritual ordering of nonordinary knowledge is an experience that all peoples, past, present and to come have in common."

Terry Tafoya explains that stories plant symbols in the listeners' unconscious minds. Over time, these symbols grow to a new meaning to the listener, giving intuitive insight to the rational mind, and a focus for emotional growth. Tellers need not end a story with "the moral of this story is" since the metaphors and symbols are planted in the unconscious mind. I was always captivated as a child by the symbol of the glass hill in the Cinderlad story. I can hear some readers chuckle. I don't think it was phallic. It was shiny, and I thought the Princess must have looked pretty atop the glass hill with three golden apples on her lap. The image of the glass hill may first have been simply a shiny, glittery symbol to me, but over time, that image grew into a symbol of purity of purpose and the hope to strive for one's best as an adult. These seeds of symbols and metaphors grow into strength in goals over time.

Metaphors and symbols talk to the non-rational unconscious mind and as such can enhance non-rational learning. Richard Restak reports that only 10 percent of the brain's six billion neurons and one hundred trillion neural connections are used by the conscious mind. This means the unconscious accounts for a vast proportion of the total brain mass. If the unconscious can be accessed for learning and healing, then humans can tap more potential. Since metaphors are processed in the non-rational unconscious parts of the brain, using metaphors in stories allows us to actually communicate "underneath" the limited frames of reference in the conscious mind, speeding a transformation of consciousness and thus opening the inner world to deep wisdom.

Stories Are Transformational

"A treasure-trove of imaginative powers lives within us all. These powers often lie stunted and dormant, yet to awake the pictures that live in our story-imagination is to become more fully and radiantly alive…. Above all, storytelling gives us love and courage for life."
-Nancy Mellon

Nancy Mellon is a storyteller, prolific writer, and disseminator of the healing quality of story. She was a former Waldorf teacher. Waldorf Schools are based on the philosophy of Rudolf Steiner, an Austrian genius, philosopher, and social reformer of the late nineteenth century. At that time, a social movement was growing across Europe to educate the children of workers, when education had been reserved for the rich. The owners of the Waldorf-Astoria cigarette plant in Stuttgart, Germany, contacted Steiner to set up a school for the children of the plant's workers. His idea was to awaken children's supersensible perception with story, art, crafts, movement, and relationships. Teachers tell stories, re-creating ancient cultural and historical accounts. Gregory Cajete notes:

Stories present deep insights into the affective dimension of human learning, socialization in community, and the role of story in the transfer of cultural knowledge and values. The deep psychological mechanisms associated with myths, stories, and storytelling facilitate the development of not only self-knowledge but also social and communal knowledge on the part of children. Story is one of the most basic ways that the human brain structures and relates human experience. Everything that humans do and experience revolves around some kind of story.

Researchers have used storytelling to choose health amid peer pressure for destructive behaviors. By telling stories of their experiences, youth can gain strength from the cultural myths that create structure and patterns for their lives. Storytelling taps unconscious emotional material and memories that contain salient content about an event. As I write, "Through metaphoric knowledge stories are maps about life. These maps show what qualities create what events."

Characters in stories go through tests and transform; they can change from one thing to another. Nancy Mellon shows how the wisdom of paradoxical thinking is conveyed through stories. Humans have both light and darkness in their nature, and stories do not shy away from the adversity of life. The ability to think in paradoxes is one of the hallmarks of wisdom, as it allows a person to hold both opposites in the mind at the same time. In Nancy Mellon's chart below, a character can be simultaneously awkward and graceful, modeling to the listener that one can be fluid between these two poles. This lets the mind be fluid between opposites. Through listening to stories and identifying with archetypal characters, listeners can open the inner world to wisdom.

CHARACTER TRANSFORMATION	
Passivity	Hope
Sloth	Industry
Loneliness	Oneness
Stubbornness	Kindness
Impatience	Forbearance
Illness	Health
Handicap	Gift
Poverty	Wealth/Contentment
Awkwardness	Grace
Rage	Attention
Vanity/Pride	Understanding
Hyperactivity	Calm
Powerlessness	Potency
Confusion	Clarity
Addition	Spiritual Illumination

Lying	Courage for the Truth
Violence	Gentleness
Obsession	Openness
Bitterness	Tastefulness
Emptiness	Fullness
Fear	Courage
Stone	Music
Animal/Beast	Human Being
Scepter	Visionary Eye
Superficiality	Depth
Death	New Life

(adapted from Mellon)

Thinking in paradoxes also allows transformation of consciousness through the tension between the opposites. By allowing a great paradox to exist, it can catalyze transformation. The mind experiences the tension and resolves it with new insight. One of my favorite Tibetan deities is Vajrasattva, known as the great purifier. He is a symbol of paradox. In one hand, he holds a bell that represents the feminine, and in the other a Vajra, or thunderbolt, for the masculine. The fact that he is holding both symbolizes that holding paradoxes can open the inner world. Vajrasattva's opposites are similar to Jung's basic archetypes of the female, the male, and the shadow. Possibly with Vajrasattva, he himself is the shadow or the unknown void.

Joseph Campbell says that paradox is the key concept of the hero's journey in the myths he gathered from around the world. Shattering paradoxes solves the dilemma of transformation. This, in essence, empties consciousness of the need to figure out what is correct from what is incorrect, right from wrong. Creating emptiness allows the complexity of consciousness to play on the screen of the mind, yielding cognitive fluidity and agility. Some of the paradoxes he documents are: the void and the world; eternity and time; truth and illusion; enlightenment and compassion; the God and the Goddess; the enemy and the friend; death and birth; subject and object; yang and yin.

125

Paradoxical thinking opens the inner world to move toward wisdom. This can lead to the other characteristics of wisdom of the ability to sense the interconnection to other life, creating the possibility of solving intractable human dilemmas. For example, in the contemporary world with climate change, wisdom is necessary to solve the overheating of the atmosphere. With increased wisdom comes transformation, and also, as we'll see below, expanded consciousness.

Storytelling and Expanded Consciousness

Expanded consciousness is a form of liminality. This is also called a liminal state in which there is a feeling of interconnectedness to other forms of creation. The experience of an energetic wholeness fills the mind-body. Sometimes expanded intelligence happens in dream states or peak experiences. In this state, ambiguity is tolerated, and judgment is suspended about what is and what is not reality. Spiritual feelings of unity occur, and insights and "ahas" may pop into the mind. By merging with the archetypal patterns during storytelling, the storyteller creates a liminal space, speaking from the heart as well as the head. This allows listeners to merge with this space and transcend normal waking consciousness. Therefore, through storytelling, a person can experience an expanded intelligence, allowing the possibility of insight. This, in turn, can fuel transformational insight by injecting new awareness into the individual's consciousness.

Chapter Six: The Storytelling Virtues

The Storytelling Five Virtues

When people embody storytelling virtues, it will lead to wisdom. The heroes and heroines in stories map life's adversity, find helpers, and bring back gifts for themselves and others. Stories show the gifts can be tangible, but more often, they are changes in the main character's awareness. During the journey of story, characters find a quality they can value and incorporate into their lives. The storytelling virtues are guideposts, qualities to embody to open the inner world to wisdom.

With my background of using the wheel as an organizing tool for balance and harmony, I developed a way to communicate the definition of storytelling virtues. Recall that the wheels were initially created by humans to align human activity to the creative forces that propel Earth's movement around the Sun. The concept was that the forces that kept Earth on its orbit were powerful and creative. Creating wheels allowed humans to align with this creativity. I thought it would make sense to use the wheel to organize the virtues. The wheel can only turn when it is balanced. A person gains energy when each of the points in the wheel is attended to. People can open to their inner worlds of holism. Just as the story cycle is a wheel, the virtues can conform to a wheel.

Let's look in brief at the five storytelling virtues on this wheel with some story examples. We will explore them in more depth in the rest of the book.

THE STORYTELLING
FIVE VIRTUES

Storytelling Virtue: Acceptance

In the east, or the beginning, heroes and heroines in stories face a call to adventure. Their lives have progressed at a steady pace, but something changes. In some cases, the change is dramatic. This has been termed "the call to adventure." Instead of struggling with the change or denying it, the main character at some point realizes the change is inescapable and moves to acceptance. The following excerpts from the stories showcase such acceptance.

One of the stories that really showcases acceptance is Ganesha's story. In his story, humility is a key to embracing the adversity that life presents. The elephant-headed Hindu deity must accept that he has lost his human head. He shows humility in accepting his lot and becoming the remover of obstacles, and he learns to bestow beneficence on new endeavors.

In the story *The Children*, the parents need to exercise acceptance in realizing that they have made a mistake in abandoning the wise woman after she helped them become pregnant. They realize they have to cooperate with the wise woman to maintain the health of their families. The parents reach out to get healing herbs from the elder who lives near the village first to overcome their infertility. They soon forgot about her. But then they learn they have to accept their responsibility in cooperating to take care of the elder when they need her to give them another herb to heal their sick children.

Avalokiteśvara, the Tibetan Buddha of compassion, models doubt that often comes before acceptance. He is overcome with doubt as he experiences the pain in the human condition that he cannot relieve. He has doubts about completing his bodhisattva mission of relieving suffering when he sees so much suffering in the human condition. His head breaks into many pieces. He accepts he can't do the work alone, and the Buddha in the Pure Land gives him eleven heads and one thousand arms to realize he has help.

Storytelling Virtue: Tests

I've placed the theme of tests at the south of the wheel. The south represents making a living and a purposeful activity. When the sun is high, the hero and heroine learn that there will be tests, since difficulty and adversity are unavoidable in life. To navigate the tests, the characters must learn skills, find and strengthen character traits, and accept help. Herein lies the true wisdom of stories. Tests come, and characters find ways through them. The point here is that after accepting the change, a test will come, and stories show tried and true ways of facing adversity.

In Ramayana's story, he faces much negativity. He is denied his throne, and a demoness tries to seduce him. When she is unsuccessful, his betrothed is kidnapped. He faces many, many tests. One of his father's wives manipulates the father to make her own son king even though it is Ramayana's right. He faces demons in the woods and has to fight a ten-headed monster after Sita, his fiancée, is kidnapped. His many tests are metaphors of the adversity all humans face.

In the story *Keep on Steppin'*, Dave faces the tests of physical abuse and the loss of freedom. Dave's tests are life-threatening. He is a slave in the South before the Civil War. Dave earns his freedom by saving Massa's children. But he has to work an extra year, and as he was finally leaving, Massa tries to use guilt to keep him from leaving, saying all the family loves him. But Dave faced the tests, worked diligently for a year, and then he kept on walking.

In the story *The Dragon's Robe*, Kwan Yin faces the test of spotting deceit. She is an orphan, and as a weaver, she travels to the Emperor's home amid a famine to win a position in the kingdom. Kwan Yin faces many tests after coming across an Old Man who needs help. While taking care of him, he put her through many tests to watch the lords who were to place sacred objects on an altar. Kwan Yin reported that they stole the objects, and the Old Man exhorts her to keep weaving. She navigates both tests and helps the Emperor defeat the lords to claim his throne.

In the creation story *The Four Directions*, the peoples of the four directions must face the test of overcoming jealousy to share their gifts and learn from each other. In the Hopi story, the Creator makes peoples for each of the four directions with special gifts, unique unto themselves. The tests for the peoples are to go out on their migrations and overcome their jealousy and pettiness to learn from the peoples different from them.

In my story *Sophia and Claude*, Sophia must face the test to live with the vegetarian dragon Claude to find the truth. This story was created for a nurses' workshop to show that the unconscious was a friendly place with healing power. The multiracial woman, Sophia, risks all to become a sacrifice to a dragon to learn the truth. Her tests involve staying with the dragon for ten years. She and the dragon break the cycle of sacrificing women to keep the peace.

Storytelling Virtue: Bravery

As the heroes and heroines accept that the "normal" of their lives has fundamentally changed, they draw on their bravery. Being brave is essential to face changes and adversity and to look for helpers within and without. Part of bravery is having the humility to accept help. In stories, characters pull on their inner resources as the tests emerge. One of their consistent inner resources is bravery. Often, even when characters are introverts or a bit timid, they find that they can be brave.

I've placed this virtue in the west of the wheel. Imagine a sunset on the ocean with colors of gold and even violet. It prompts reflection and calm. It can be a time for introspection to find bravery within. The theme of bravery teaches that it is a human's capability.

Isis shows bravery to take flight to find her dead husband, Osiris. As a member of a quintuplet, she is married to one brother, Osiris. Their other brother, Seth, kills Osiris out of jealousy. She flies to find Osiris's body on a sand bank in the Nile, mating with him to birth Horus. She is also brave enough to trick the sun god Re into telling her his name and granting the sun's power to her.

Lilith, as Adam's first wife, stood up to both God and Adam, saying she did not want to be subservient. She was thrown out of Eden, but she brought knowledge to humans by transforming into the snake to tempt Eve. Courage and bravery go hand in hand in Lilith's story.

Gaia's story shows that bravery comes in many forms. In Gaia's case, she was crafty to save lives from the patriarchy, even when the patriarchy was her mate and her son. Gaia is the Earth mother, and as such, she acts to protect life. Being the original feminist, she fought with bravery against her mate, Ouranos, and then her son, Cronos. She stood up to Cronos even though he was the one who helped her stand up to his father. Ouranos wanted to eat their ugly children, and Gaia had Cronos give him stones to eat instead. She then supported Zeus, Cronos's son, in killing his father so that Cronos would not kill his own children to keep the throne.

Bravery comes in the form of a man being willing to keep his family in *Buffalo Woman*. In this story, the hunter has married a beautiful woman from the Buffalo Tribe, but his tribe is cruel to her. She returns to her tribe, turning back into a buffalo. The hunter shows great bravery in tracking her and his son, Calf Boy. Eventually, he has to face death and rebirth to reunite with his family.

Storytelling Virtue: Beauty

Completing the round of the wheel is beauty in the north. The north is a time of celebrating spirit in nature, such as looking at the Milky Way in the midnight sky. Having accepted the change in circumstances, faced tests, and owned their bravery, heroes and heroines can now contemplate beauty. Beauty enriches the soul and fills the space purified by pain. Beauty is a motivator to find the deep, gentle velvet in the heart. Beauty gives the experience of interconnection.

Beauty pervades *The White Spider*. In the story, beauty includes humility, loyalty, and friendship. Piki is a poor man working in subsistence farming along a rainforest river in Uruguay. He falls in love with the Chieftain's beautiful daughter and only wins her when his friend, the White Spider, weaves a gorgeous lace shawl. Piki's humility is beautiful. The Chieftain's daughter is a beauty, and the lace made by the White Spider is beautiful.

It might be a stretch of the imagination to consider beauty when thinking of Coyote's story. But amid Coyote's failings, the beauty is that he affirms himself throughout his humiliations and failures. His irrepressible resiliency is a beautiful thing in and of itself. Even though in this story Coyote has successfully brought a kill home to feed his pups, he continues to be jealous of other animals and their fine attributes, claws, fur, and tails. He wallows in self-pity even when Owl tells him he is the best at being crafty with humans. In the end, Coyote affirms his own view of himself and is ready for another day.

In *Juan Bobo,* his innocence exudes beauty. Juan Bobo's story is in the genre of Coyote stories; after all, "Bobo" means fool, and Coyote is often foolish in his tales. Juan follows his mother's instructions to the letter, but he ends up offending people and getting into trouble. For example, when he sees a wedding party, he says, "My deepest condolences." He says this since the only procession he has seen before was a funeral. But he learns from his mistakes, and in the end, he inadvertently scares thieves and takes gold home to his mother. Juan radiates the beauty of innocence by embodying it and seeing that in others.

Storytelling Virtue: Death/Rebirth

Through stories, heroes and heroines are transformed, which is represented at times by the metaphor of death and rebirth. For example, Jonah is swallowed by the whale, a metaphoric death, and there is a rebirth as he emerges changed. Story characters are ultimately changed through a cycle to emerge in a new state. Sometimes the main characters face death, sometimes they die and are reborn, and sometimes they actually die. Death can bring life to and inspire others.

John the True dies out of loyalty to his King, but he is reborn. Even though there is a King, Queen, and their two sons in *John the True*, John is truly the protagonist. He has special abilities, such as the ability to understand animal language. When he heeds some crows' warnings of the King and Queen's possible demise, he risks his own life by warning them. He is turned to stone when he divulges the warning he received to the King. But through the Queen's dreams, she brings him back to life with the blood of the dragon that John slew to save them. Facing death, John personifies bravery, courage, and loyalty, inspiring the King's twin sons.

In Deirdre's tragic story, death abounds. Even though there is no rebirth, she dies well. Trees grow from her and her lover's graves to unite, showing the enduring power of love. The King had discovered Deirdre in the woods, where her father had cloistered her, due to the prophecy that she would be the cause of the death of two kings. After the King forced her to promise to marry him, she met her true love, Naoise. After Deirdre and Naoise run away to Scotland with his two brothers, the King tricks them into returning to his land, using sorcery to kill Naoise and the brothers. Unable to bear the pain, Deirdre throws herself into Naoise's grave and dies. The King does not let them be buried together, but a tree grows out of each grave, and they join to create a heart. Their deaths convey the ultimate value of love and confirm the refusal to be controlled by evil forces.

Now let's turn to look at the stories of each virtue in more detail.

Chapter Seven: The Virtue of Acceptance

Of the storytelling virtues, acceptance is the first. As noted earlier, I've put it in the east on the wheel, showing the beginning, the dawn. Acceptance is the beginning of opening the mind to inner wisdom.

I like to use the 1996 movie *Independence Day,* starring Will Smith, to exemplify a sudden change in circumstances. The movie starts with Will Smith in bed with his wife and then having breakfast. It is a homey, stable scene. He is a pilot in the armed services, and as he goes out to his car, eerie music plays. Then he is called up to confront the alien ship. Adventure calls, and nothing is the same. In stories, the main character has a choice to accept change, fight it, or deny it. Sometimes, time is needed for acceptance to sink in.

The stages of grief, as defined in Richard Edlich and Elisabeth Kübler-Ross's article, are denial, anger, bargaining, depression, and acceptance—acceptance is the final stage. But in story, acceptance is the first stage and maybe the most difficult. However, the grief process demonstrates that acceptance can take time. Moving through all the stages can take a long time, but in stories, heroes and heroines don't have such a privilege. Sometimes acceptance needs to happen swiftly. One technique from Zen Buddhism is "accepting what is" and not arguing with what life brings you. Also, Gestalt psychologist Fritz Perls' dictum is to accept something before it can change.

Ganesha

Ganesha is a profound story of acceptance. His story is one of my favorites, as Ganesha is such a friendly deity, the elephant Hindu god. Ganesha not only has a story but also is a revered deity. He is the center of a ten-day celebration, known as Ganesh Chaturthi or Vinayaka Chaturi, in the Indian state of Maharashtra. Families have Ganesha statues in their homes and temples, and they are carried through the streets. People throw red sandalwood powder on the statues and on each other. It is a joyous celebration that conveys the elixir of life that Ganesha exudes.

Ganesha's tale follows the story cycle. Ganesha is the son of Parvati and Shiva. Shiva is one of the Hindu pantheon triumvirate: Shiva, the destroyer; Brahma, the unknowable; and Vishnu, the preserver. The idea of a destroyer might be a negative notion, but out of destruction can come new life. A good metaphor for Shiva might be a volcano. The eruption of the volcano destroys the land around the volcano, and out of the destruction comes regeneration. Volcanic ash becomes a fertile medium for new life to sprout. Shiva is a progenitor of life after volatile destruction.

I've referred to his story before, but in more detail we understand Ganesha's ultimate acceptance of his transition from man to elephant deity. The story goes that Parvati, Shiva's consort, wanted to bathe calmly. She asked Ganesha to stand outside the bath and keep his dad, Shiva, out, as his amorous advances could be distracting. Shiva came, and Ganesha stood up to his ferocious dad. Incensed, Shiva took his head. Parvati came out of the bath and yelled at Shiva, and she forced him to find a new head for Ganesha. A servant found the nearest head, which was from an elephant. Thus, Ganesha was created.

There is not much in recorded fables about Ganesha's life before becoming a revered deity. But clearly, he accepted his transition. He accepted physical, emotional, and spiritual trauma. He even lost his life as a human. Through the acceptance of his situation, he transcended the trauma or possibly incorporated the karma. Instead of becoming a destroyer like his father, he grew to represent beneficence and new beginnings. Through the humility of his acceptance, he gave grace to hundreds of thousands of people. As elephants can move logs, Ganesha can remove life's obstacles. Acceptance is the virtue to start this process.

The Children

I've talked about this story a number of times. I find it multi-layered with many lessons from the wise elder. The Yoruba tale of *The Children* offers many lessons of acceptance. In terms of the story cycle, acceptance is extremely important at two points in the cycle of this story. First, after the call to adventure, when the village couples cannot conceive, the main characters have to come to grips with the fact that their reality is fundamentally changed. This is a difficult task. Humans seek homeostasis; they keep things the same unless there is a reason for changing. Jean Piaget, the famous child psychologist, developed a theory to explain how children's thinking skills change to become more logical. At first, children think magically. Later, they are fooled by what they see, saying that a lump of clay looks like more if it is shaped to look taller. Still later, children's cognitive schemas change so that they can make logical deductions.

As a young man, Jean Piaget was interested in biology as he studied mollusks. He knew the biological principle of homeostasis: that a natural system will seek to stay the same unless a change is introduced. He applied this to how children's cognition changes. New information that refutes how they thought the world works shifts this homeostasis. They accommodate the new information to form a more inclusive cognitive schema of how the world works. In story, the call to adventure is a fundamental shift in homeostasis, and accepting this is a hard task.

This principle of homeostasis works throughout the natural world. Nothing changes unless there is something that shifts the balance. The reason stories are transformational is that a new situation presents itself, and the status quo is no longer normal. In stories, characters often have no choice but to change. Most of the time, the changes are outside of the main character's control, and acceptance is the only way forward.

Stories are metaphors for human life. The call to adventure happens many times to people. Life throws curveballs, and people are thrown for a loop. Without change, people stay in homeostasis. Acceptance of the change allows the character to embrace or at least come to grips with the change to move to the next storytelling virtue, that of tests. This may take a bit of time, but to complete the cycle, acceptance is the key.

There are two distinct times in *The Children* when acceptance is difficult but necessary. The first one happens when couples from a supposedly idyllic village cannot conceive children. Their normal reality changed. They had thought that they could marry and children would come naturally to bring joy and to sustain the village. But when they couldn't conceive, they came to acceptance quickly. The villagers remembered that there was an elder who lived outside of the village who was wise in the way of medicinal plants. She gave them herbs, and lo and behold, children were conceived. The villagers helped the elder monthly, making repairs and tilling her garden. But time went on. Complacency returned. They returned to their homeostatic reality. They forgot the elder, and in effect, they failed the test of the storytelling cycle.

But a new call to adventure emerged. The children became ill, and acceptance of the new reality came quickly since they were distraught with worry for their children. Again, they went to their elder. Not only did they accept that they needed to act, but also that they needed to ask for help. Part of acceptance is humility. When the call to adventure comes and one's reality is rocked, it takes humility to realize that one has to change things. Machismo or toughing it out won't work. Something has to give. The villagers went with their tails tucked in their behinds to ask for help. Her herbs worked again, and this time the villagers passed the test. They kept their adventure to face the tests: commitment to help the elder monthly. The second time, they accepted the change quickly.

Avalokiteśvara

Avalokiteśvara's story shows the acceptance of things one cannot deal with. In his case, he couldn't cope with the enormity of human suffering. Avalokiteśvara was a bodhisattva. In Tibetan Buddhism, a bodhisattva is a person who has reached enlightenment but decides not to enter nirvana until all sentient life can do so. Enlightenment is the goal of becoming one with spirit through meditation and other practices. If enlightenment or nirvana is achieved, then the cycle of reincarnation is broken, and one can move into the Pure Land. However, a bodhisattva says, "I won't move on to nirvana. I will stay on the earth and work until all sentient beings are saved."

Avalokiteśvara traveled around the earth, acting to relieve human suffering. One day, when he was picking up a dying man on the road, he gave up. Distraught, he threw his hands up almost like Jesus did on the cross, "Why me, God?" At that point, his head broke into pieces, and he was transported to the Pure Land. He saw with his spiritual eyes, even though his head had been destroyed. He saw the Buddha, and the Buddha gave him eleven heads and a thousand arms to do the work of relieving suffering. Avalokiteśvara was transformed. He had to accept that he couldn't relieve all suffering by himself. He had to embrace the humility that he could just do what was in front of him. Although he had great gifts to do the work—eleven heads and a thousand arms—he could only do his part. Again, humility was an essential component to his being able to accept change and navigate through it.

Chapter Eight: The Virtue of Tests

On the wheel of storytelling virtues, after acceptance in the east comes tests in the south. This is a storytelling virtue that creates a liminal space to open the inner world of wisdom. As people accept the new normal, a fundamental change in their lives, the next turn of the wheel is that tests will come. Acceptance allows a person to be ready for tests. If people know that there will be tests after acceptance, then they can be ready and look for the helpers who will assist people in surviving and possibly thriving through those tests. This wisdom is that tests will inevitably happen in life.

Many people live in denial that they will not have tests in life. If adversity comes, people embodying the storytelling virtue of acceptance won't say, "Why did this happen to me?" They will be agile and ready for the ambiguity of what lies ahead. Tests are part of the reality of life, and the key is to be ready to accept them. There are ups and downs in life. And the amazing thing is that acceptance sets the stage to face tests and use them for transformation. The main characters in stories are sometimes reluctant to face tests, as we all are. However, others may embrace them, knowing that tests are inevitable. By acknowledging the reality of tests, a person can be open to what may come and be ready to look for the helpers available to navigate them.

Ramayana

Ramayana is an ancient Hindu story stemming from the seventh century BCE. It's a compilation of stories found in the *Rig Veda*, the ancient Sanskrit text consisting of over 24,000 verses, and is considered the first poem of India. The story abounds with tests, including but not exclusively the loss of a rightful crown, attacks by demons, the kidnapping of a beloved, the death of a loved one, and a battle with a ten-headed demon.

To make sense of the story, it is good to review its characters.

- **Rama:** the eldest son of a King who is the rightful heir but has been passed over because of manipulation by one of the King's wives. Rama elects to go to the wilderness after he loses the throne.
- **Lakshmana:** Rama's favorite brother, who goes into the wilderness with him.
- **Sita:** Rama's betrothed, who goes into the wilderness too.
- **Ravana:** a ten-headed demon who has a kingdom on an island. This island is thought to be Sri Lanka. Ravana kidnaps Sita to avenge his sister, who Lakshmana wounded. Ravana's sister was in love with Rama and tried to hurt Sita.
- **Shurpanakha:** Ravana's sister who wants to marry Rama but is wounded by Lakshmana.
- **Hanuman:** A winged-monkey warrior who helps Rama defeat Ravana.

I pick up the plot of this story after Rama's father, the King, has allowed one of his wives to advocate for her son, manipulating the King into passing the throne on to him instead of Rama. Rama was a standup guy and said, "Okay, I'll yield, and I'll go into the wilderness," demonstrating the storytelling wisdom of acceptance. His brother, Lakshmana, and his betrothed, Sita, go to the wilderness with him. But all things were not good for Rama. <u>Shurpanakha, a demoness, the sister of the ten-headed demon Ravana, saw Rama in the forest and fell in love with him.</u> She met Lakshmana and said she would eat Sita so that she could have Rama. The brother cut off the demoness's ears and nose. For revenge, Shurpanakha bewitched her brother, Ravana, a ten-headed demon, into falling in love with Sita. As a result, he kidnapped Sita, taking her to his island kingdom.

Rama and Lakshmana go all out to find Sita. They are told about a monkey kingdom, and when they visit, the brothers are called on to defeat the Monkey King's brother. In gratitude, the Monkey King assigns his best warrior, Hanuman, to help Rama. After many searches, a vulture tells Hanuman where to find Sita. A great battle ensues. Lakshmana is mortally wounded, and Hanuman flies to the mountains to bring back a healing herb to save him. In the final throes of the battle, Rama and Ravana face off. A sage appears to Rama and tells him to use the power of the Sun. Using this information, Rama harnesses the Sun and shoots a fatal arrow into Ravana. Rama, Sita, and Lakshmana return to their home kingdom. The brother who was given the throne earlier relinquishes it to Rama. The rightful King, Rama, takes his place on the throne.

There is a sexist part of this story that I'll just note here, because I'm uncomfortable with it. After Rama rescues Sita, she has the shame that Ravana may have spoiled her in the sexual sense. She stands forth and says, "If I am not pure, may the earth take me." The earth opens up under Sita, but instead of taking her, it shoots her back up to be standing with the group. This part of the story is supportive of Sita, but the fact that she had to be ready to sacrifice herself with the notion that she might be impure is too much for me. I'm not sure I have the right to change the story, but I think stories evolve in their telling.

One thing to note in this story is that the tests are life-threatening, existential, and in some instances, even supernatural. In everyday lives, tests may not be so desperate, but for even smaller ups and downs, how characters face and navigate tests has wisdom for humans.

For his first test, Rama accepted his situation. In fact, he embraced it. Even though it was his right to have the throne, he took the noble course of moving into the wilderness instead of taking advantage of the cushy existence as the rightful heir to his father's throne. He let go of material comfort and immersed himself in the unknowns of the forest. It is not clear to me that Rama knew he would have helpers with the tests ahead. It appears that he embraced the reality of his life, or as we say in Zen, accepted what is. No longer an heir to the throne, he was on his own—a difficult thing to accept—whatever awaited him. But with Rama's integrity and stellar moral fortitude, fate gave him a good turn. That is a lesson here: If one stays with one's values, then one is more ready to see the helpers within and without. Rama discovers that he will find help in his new situation. His brother, Lakshmana, has come to support him. His betrothed, Sita, followed him. When Sita is taken by Ravana, Hanuman, the winged monkey, helps him. The Sun even helps Rama make a true shot. The art of embracing tests is to look around for helpers. Those might be tools and skills, people lending a hand, or inner strength and character strengths.

Rama had many inner and external characteristics that came to his aid: courage to accept his fate, perseverance to withstand his isolation, bravery to face dangerous situations, faith in his friends, openness to supernatural help, and humility in accepting help. He also obviously had physical gifts—his skill with a bow and arrow, for example. He had the help of his betrothed and his brother. He had spiritual help in the vision of the sage in his battle with Ravana. He had the inner attitude of "accepting what is." Instead of arguing with what was happening, being in denial about it, or asking Job's question, "Why me?" he accepted what was in front of him.

I had a friend once who had difficulties. She had lost jobs and was focused on a married man. She consistently bemoaned that she couldn't be with him: "Why won't he leave his wife and be with me?" She consistently denied reality and actually argued with it. To accept reality and realize that there may be difficulty ahead—or tests—is a virtue to embody that is taught by story. This achieves Thomas Aquinas's lifeability, or making one's life work. Inner characteristics, resources, hidden character traits, loved ones, or strangers ready to help can all be available to aid you in facing and navigating the tests.

Keep on Steppin'

The African American folktale, *Keep on Steppin'* also showcases tests for the main character, Dave. This is one of my favorite stories, and I return to it many times in this book. I tell it in the most detail here.

Dave was slaving on a plantation somewhere in Tennessee. He was in the field one day and saw a terrible sight. Ol' Massa and Ol' Missy's children were out in a boat on the river that ran close to the plantation's land, and they had lost their oars. The boat was out of control, spinning around. Dave cried, "Someone help them." Another slave, High John, yelled, "Leave them alone. White people beat us; we don't need to help them." But Dave decided to help. He ran to the lake, dived in, and swam to the boat, bringing it back to the bank.

Missy and Massa ran to the bank, and they were mighty happy to have their children back. Massa said, "You're the best slave we have, and after a good crop filling up the barn, I'll give you freedom." Dave had to hoe and plant for a year, and finally, the whole barn was filled with a good crop. He was ready to go, but Massa said to him, "Don't leave. The children love you. I love you. Don't leave." But Dave tied the new clothes Massa gave him in a bundle, putting it on a stick, and threw it over his shoulder. Massa kept yelling at him. "We all love you. Missy loves you. The children love you." Then he went low and said, "You're still a slave even though you are free."

Dave faced fundamental tests. Of course, the most fundamental was being a slave. A part of this was being owned by someone, being beaten, being told where to show up each day, being told who his mate was, and always being subjected to the whim of his master. I don't think many of us could relate to such profound depravity of human humiliation, suffering, and abuse. This might be the most egregious test of all—human slavery. Dave had persevered and figured out how to stay alive amid ultimate human degradation. When the children of his Massa were at risk, other slaves told him to leave them to die. But Dave had an inner sense of morality, and he decided to save the children's lives, swimming out to move the boat to safety.

Afterward, Massa said he would give Dave freedom, but he had to fill the barn with the next crop before he could leave. When he was being released, Massa and his family tried to use the guilt card to keep him there, another test. Dave knew that this was not real love. It was a manipulation to keep him in slavery.

Dave faced his tests with many internal characteristics. Perseverance was the foremost. He knew he had to persevere until the crops were in. Second was his moral compass. He was going to save the White children even though the White Massa persecuted him in slavery. The reward for this characteristic was ultimately his freedom. Another characteristic was his mental clarity. He knew that Massa meant him no good, telling him that he and his family loved him. He had to ignore this manipulation. Through these internal characteristics, he found the strength to keep on steppin'. The situation of the children being in danger was a helper in giving him the chance to act on his values. There were no external helpers for Dave. It was all his inner fortitude.

The Dragon's Robe

I don't want to belabor this story, but returning to it shows that *The Dragon's Robe* is an excellent example of the storytelling virtue of tests. I tell it in detail here. *The Dragon's Robe* is a contemporary children's book that uses Kwan Yin as the main character. Kwan Yin is a Buddhist deity in the story. She is the Chinese expression of Avalokiteśvara, the Buddha of compassion. Therefore, any story about Kwan Yin could be significant in understanding compassion. In the mythic realm of storytelling, metaphors are connected even though they may not be consciously chosen by their authors—they may rely less on logic than intuition. So, by using Kwan Yin's name, the storyteller brings Kwan Yin's archetypal characteristic, compassion, to face her tests.

The tests in *The Dragon's Robe* are profoundly dangerous to Kwan Yin's well-being. First, she becomes an orphan and poor amid a famine in China. She must travel from village to village with her loom on her back, weaving silks into fabric with beautiful colors—vermillion, emerald, green, or bright yellow. As with *Ramayana*, her story is a bit complicated, and a review of the characters helps see the tests she faced and the helpers inside and outside of her.

- **Kwan Yin:** a young, orphaned woman, a weaver, living in poverty. She learned that the Emperor was granting safe haven to the poor amid a famine, provided they could travel to the capital.
- **Old Man:** a sick man who Kwan Yin helps after discovering him on her travels.

- **Lord Phoenix, Overseer of the Emperor's rice fields:** He is asked to put the golden rice on the Dragon's altar, but steals it instead and brings on the burning of all the rice fields.
- **Lord Tiger, General of the Emperor's army:** He is asked to put the golden knife on the Dragon's altar, but steals it instead, starting the invasion of China by Khan's army.
- **Khan:** Mongol leader who invaded China.

Kwan Yin's first test was that she was an orphan. Her next test was that even though she gained skills as an apprentice weaver and could make a living as an itinerant, there was a famine, and no one wanted a weaver. The test of poverty and lack of food haunted her. Heading for a safe haven with the Emperor, her next test was to travel a long journey that included climbing a mountain to get to the Emperor's palace. She starts weaving a beautiful silk robe featuring a dragon. She thinks this is a fitting gift for the Emperor, and she continues weaving on her stops along her journey. The tests continue. After starting her climb up the mountain, she finds a sick Old Man who needs water and care. This is another test: to choose to continue the journey for her own safety or to act in compassion. Her compassion is a helper. She stops to help the Old Man, and he tells her to continue her weaving.

The Old Man lives close to a dragon's temple. Lord Phoenix and Lord Tiger visit the Old Man, and he gives each of them something to put on the altar of the temple. Lord Phoenix is to put a kernel of golden rice, but he steals it instead. Lord Tiger is to put a knife on the altar, and he steals it. The Old Man asks Kwan Yin to observe them as they go to the temple to supposedly follow his instructions. Lord Phoenix's action intensifies the famine, and Lord Tiger's action creates a great fire ripping through the country. As a result, the Mongol leader Khan invades the country. Amid all this, Kwan Yin keeps on weaving because she still wants to find a haven with the Emperor. As these disasters beset the country, she finishes the dragon robe. When the Old Man puts it on, he is transformed into the Emperor, and he defeats the Khan and restores the fields to grow rice.

Her helpers were many and included her skills as a weaver, her compassion to help the Old Man, her perseverance to keep on weaving amid threats by powerful Lords, and her bravery in making a long voyage. Also, she had the encouragement from the Old Man, who turned out to be the Emperor. It is true that the Emperor tricked her by posing as a sick old man and that he talked her into staying and taking care of him instead of going to the Emperor's haven. He also employed her as his spy when he sent Lord Phoenix and then Lord Tiger to place items on the altar. Kwan Yin's interaction with the Old Man/Emperor could be seen as one sustained test with three steps. The sub-steps were first, to interrupt her journey to safety to help a dying Old Man; second, to take the direction by the Old Man to spy on two powerful lords; and third, to keep weaving the Emperor's robe amid threats by Lord Phoenix, Lord Tiger, and the invasion of Khan's army.

After Kwan Yin met these tests and the Emperor was restored to himself by donning the robe she had woven, he then clothed her in a golden robe and took her to his court. The Emperor said, "Thank you, Kwan Yin. You have taught me to trust a poor weaver over my selfish Lords. Come live in my palace and help me remember what I have learned."

Kwan Yin's heroine's journey exemplifies many elements of the quality of tests that occur in life, and also the variety of helpers. Tests are fundamentally difficult, as in life and death; thus, tests can be profoundly central to survival. Humans idealize what their future might be with no bumps and only happiness, but part of life is hardships and difficulties. It is not all of life, as human existence also includes joy, bliss, calm, and boredom—the whole continuum of emotions and states of consciousness. What story wisdom teaches is that even though there are tests, there are inner and outer helpers to assist one through the tests.

In Kwan Yin's case, inner qualities were central, including the physical strength to hike, the artistry of weaving, compassion to help the Old Man/Emperor, spying skills to observe the Lords at the Dragon's Shrine, the perseverance to keep weaving amid profound danger, and confidence. External helpers included her weaving teacher early in life and the Old Man/Emperor.

The Four Directions

As noted earlier, I worked from 1986 to 1998 as the Director of the Center for Indian Bilingual Teacher Education (CIBTE) at Prescott College in Prescott, Arizona. In that job, I was on a quest to learn to be culturally competent and to work respectfully and successfully to help American Indian teacher aides get their BA degrees and earn Arizona teaching credentials. I criticized Eurocentric curriculum that excluded other ways of knowing, and I saw CIBTE as a chance to learn from and collaborate with tribal education directors to build a program that was inclusive of learners' cultures.

Some scholars throw around the term "hegemony," meaning that the dominant culture—for example, White upper-class cultural values—permeates the education system. Cultural competence, at least for education, centers on the idea that intelligence and learning modes are culturally relative. For example, indigenous Australian people consider intelligence as valuing the learning of experiential exploration in the outback. Being able to notice the difference in the texture and nuances of a stone is an example of intelligence. Intelligence to indigenous Australians is successfully adapting to the environment or mapping travel in the outback. In Eurocentric, or Western, cultural perspective, including North America and Europe, being logical is considered a sign of intelligence. Both are intelligences, since they are successful adaptations to the environment. Intelligence is culturally inflected.

I have worked in many diverse communities over the years. As a graduate student, I was a consultant in an urban elementary school district in Indianapolis, Indiana, and I conducted workshops in the Bronx and Philadelphia as well as for the northern Cheyenne and Hopi peoples. I started the CIBTE at Prescott College for twenty-two tribes in Arizona. I had a Fulbright in India, teaching curriculum design. Then I started a non-profit for substance abuse prevention on the Tohono O'odham Indian Nation in Southern Arizona and later also served Latinx youth in Phoenix, Arizona. As part of that work, I was struck by the cultural differences in how people learn and define knowledge.

Epistemology is the field of philosophy that studies human methods of knowing. Being captivated by Southwest Indian culture and their methods of knowing, I organized a conference on Native American epistemology. While traveling around the Navajo (Diné) and Hopi nations, as well as other nations in Arizona, I had heard a Hopi man tell the story of migrations and recruited him for the conference. With some Native American tribes, there are seasonal restrictions on telling stories. For example, in some tribes, stories can only be told in winter, and there are restrictions on who can tell which stories. Being sensitive to cultural appropriation, I asked the man who told the story of creation if I could tell it, modifying it to my cultural background, and he agreed. Hence, I began telling the story of *The Four Directions*. It fit well into my work at that time, since I had been studying wheels around the world, and of course, the four directions are central to wheels.

In *The Four Directions* story, all the continents of the world are together in one great land mass. This fits scientific knowledge, as there was a land mass on Earth at one time called Pangaea. In the story, the Creator made people for each of the four directions, and each was given a special gift. The people were sent out to the four directions to develop their gifts, and at the end of certain cycles, maybe ten or maybe twenty-five years, the people came together in the center of Pangaea to share their gifts. This did not always go well. The people were silly, jealous, and argumentative. They argued about who had the best gift. The Creator appointed Coyote as a guardian of these gatherings. Coyote howled as the people argued, and over time, they came back into harmony and shared gifts. This went on for eons.

At a certain point, the people could not come back into balance and harmony, even as Coyote howled and howled. Then the Creator sent the people out to the four directions to develop their gifts, until they had grown and matured, so they could share. They would not see each other for a long time, and they might not even remember that the others existed.

Pangea broke up into separate continents, and the people forgot that there were other people on Earth. As time went by, people began traveling by ship, boat, and plane, and communicating by telegraph, phone, and then the internet, from continent to continent. At a certain time, some very brave individuals from each of the peoples of the four directions began congregating at a great mesa in North America. At first, the people of the four directions stayed in their separate groups. They were afraid of each other since their differences were so great. They were jealous and defensive. Humans are petty animals. But a few of the peoples of the four directions started looking at the other groups. Not only are humans argumentative, but they are also curious.

A few brave people approached each other from the four directions. Curiosity won out, and the peoples of the four directions began to learn from each other. They began to share their gifts and complete the circle. They gained strength from their differences and even developed their gifts more fully by learning from each other.

I loved this story, and since I was living in Northern Arizona, I visualized the peoples of the four directions as people from all the continents coming to a great mesa in the Four Corners region of the Colorado Plateau. I saw people from Africa, Europe, and Asia—indigenous people from throughout the world. I envisioned four camps at the foot of the mesa in the four directions. At times, they traveled to the top of the mesa and demonstrated the gifts they'd developed: art, technology, music, sacred ceremonies, and experiential and scientific wisdom.

Jealousy and arguing erupted here and there. The people of the East said, "We know more than the West, and our gifts are the best." The peoples of each direction in turn took the stage and declared themselves the best. But over time, a few brave souls quieted their pride and moved to the top of the mesa to share their gifts. The peoples of the four directions finally came back together after their long journeys to learn and share.

I love the idea that even with profound differences, people can find ways to interact with each other, cooperating to move humanity toward healing and growth. It is something I've always worked toward, trying to learn from cultures very different from my own to create environments where humans are equal around the wheel, sharing their wisdom. Differences are not minimized, but tolerance allows awareness of others.

There is a huge test in this story: the separation of the people into continents. The Creator can be seen as the helper since the Creator knew that the people needed time to develop their strengths. The test is internal as well, as the people needed to overcome jealousy and fear of their differences. Other helpers include the creativity of the people to develop their gifts and their inherent curiosity. Another helper is the strength of some of the people to overcome their jealousy and share and learn from others. The tests were navigated, and transcendence occurred with balance and harmony gained from learning all the gifts around the wheel for synergy to a new level of awareness.

Sophia and Claude

When I was studying imagery, I was very excited about psycho-neuroimmunology, and as noted earlier, I made up a story to make the unconscious friendly. Some think, probably based on Freud's work, that the unconscious is the home of the id, or base instincts, but Jung rehabilitated the personal unconscious by connecting it to the collective unconscious, the source of centuries of human experience. Thinking imagistically can have physical healing outcomes, such as increasing the number of immune T cells. The unconscious mind is active in regulating the autonomic nervous system. Using pictures or imagery, you can talk to the immune system to consciously improve immune activity. This type of functioning is usually outside of conscious control, but research shows that thinking in images, multisensory sensations such as sight, sound, smell, touch, taste, or movement can effectively communicate with the autonomic nervous system to change things like blood pressure or even cellular levels.

However, I perceived a problem in getting people to accept psychoneuroimmunology. Some people didn't believe that there is anything in the mind other than the stream of conscious thoughts. Further, relaxing and opening to the unconscious mind can seem uncomfortable to some. It can feel as if they are losing control. But Jung often said, "You run your unconscious, or it runs you." This means that if one does not open the unconscious to awareness, the unconscious mind will motivate a person in unconscious ways.

I wanted to make a story where the unconscious was a friendly place, so I decided on a vegetarian dragon with day-glow scales. I wanted to add a strong female protagonist, and the name Sophia popped into my mind. She was a multiracial woman since the time of day determined her racial identity. I made up the story of Sophia and the dragon Claude. Sophia represented the search for wisdom, and Claude, as a dragon, was the wisdom of Earth. I created a story using what I had learned about story structure and cycles from my study of imagery. I made sure to use rich sensory description.

I return to the story of Sophia and the Vegetarian Dragon, Claude, with more detail. Sophia was a bookbinder's daughter in a land that was unlike any other. There were aspects of pre-industrial civilization in her life, as she bound books by hand and wove her own clothes. But there are also futuristic elements in the story: electronic doors that are energy fields that open and close as if by magic, and electronic bulletin boards that suddenly appear or vanish, dropping from the sky. The natural world is unlike any other as well. There are mountains with rushing streams close to town with Lodgepole pines and Douglas firs, but also close were deserts with towering Saguaros topped with tiny perching Hume's owls at night.

Sophia's father is a widower, and as a devoted daughter, she worked diligently all day. She escapes to the wilderness whenever she has a break from work. She remembered finding a dog-eared copy of Clarissa Pinkola Estes's book, *Women Who Run with Wolves*, and she knew she was one of those. She loves to dance in the wilderness, and she always feels that she is a mistaken zygote, like the Ugly Duckling born in the wrong nest. She is uncomfortable in most places, but she feels she belongs in the wilderness. It is her home.

Sophia escapes to the wilderness on short breaks and at times during the day and night. There is an alpine lake that she loves because she can see her reflection and meditate. If she goes in the early morning, she can look at herself and see that her skin is like the red sandstone of the mesas below, and her hair is as black as a raven's feathers. When she goes at noon and looks at her reflection, her skin looks like the breast of a yellow thrush, and her hair is as black as ebony. If she goes in the evening at dusk, her skin appears as white as a pearl, and her hair looks like veins of gold in the earth. When she goes to the lake at midnight during a full moon, her hair looks as woolly as a sheep's coat, and her face is the color of chocolate.

Besides roaming in the wilderness, she also roams through town. She listens to the old ladies who gossip about all the young people in town, including Sophia. They say: "This girl wants to get married. That boy wants to be a football star. That Sophia, though, is different." One day, she hears them say that there will be a competition for the most successful young woman in town. Sophia had heard about the ancient Miss America contest and thought it was an exercise in sexual objectification, something that Sophia has no patience for. But she has always searched for the truth, and being successful was not the same as being sexualized. This opportunity was something out of the blue, and she knew to look for surprises. She thought she'd give it a chance. Truth could come from curious sources.

In Sophia's story, the tests came fast and furious at first, and then they came slowly after a while. After hearing the gossip about the contest, she sees on the electronic bulletin board floating in the sky in the town square: "Come to the town hall at midnight for the contest." This invitation seemed a bit foreboding, but she goes. She walks into a huge great room and sees the town council at the end of the hall. Surprised, she sees there are no other applicants. The leader says, "We've been waiting for you, Sophia. You are the most successful young woman in our village. You can bind books, hike, and take care of your father. More importantly, you are known to want to find the truth, not scurry after marriage or fame or wealth."

The leader tells her the deal: She must go to a canyon precipice to be sacrificed to a dragon. Sophia is taken aback, feeling this might be too much of a gut-wrenching test, and she wonders if she can do it. The leader continues to explain that every ten years, the town must sacrifice a young woman to keep the dragon from breathing fire and burning the village. To accept the test, she must consider whether she will risk her life. It has all the makings of a task leading to truth. Hesitantly, Sophia agrees since dragons might hold ancient wisdom.

The sacrifice day comes. A procession starts for the precipice. The village weavers have created a spectacular dress for her with all the colors of the rainbow: red, orange, yellow, green, blue, and indigo. The townsfolk accompany her and bring gifts for the dragon: vats of wine, pots overflowing with semiprecious stones, and bolts of silk. Sophia stands on the precipice looking down, and suddenly she decides maybe she should run away instead. She turns around and sees that the people from town have fled. This is another test, to face the fire-breathing dragon by herself. Something stops her from leaving. She hears a deep voice from the bottom of the canyon, saying, "Don't go. I'm lonely."

She looks down to see a bubbly creature with colors of fuchsia, turquoise, and neon green. Sophia says, "Will you eat me?"

Claude responds, "No, I'm a vegetarian."

Sophia laughs. Then, remembering her mission, she asks, "Do you know the truth?"

To this, Claude responds, "Of course, I'm a dragon. Come down and I'll tell you the truth."

Sophia changes from the beautiful rainbow dress into shorts and a T-shirt from her day pack. She dons climbing shoes, puts on her climbing gear, and turns around. Down she climbs.

Claude explains to Sophia how the silly ceremony of sacrificing a successful woman started years and years ago. On an errant flight during allergy season, Claude sneezed and burned a few fields. That had frightened the villagers. The townspeople began bringing a woman to a precipice to quell the dragon's rage. The two developed a plan: Sophia would stay with Claude for ten years, learning the truth. She would meet the procession and explain that women did not need to be sacrificed to bring peace.

Sophia takes the challenge again and stays with Claude, living in the beautiful caves of stalactites and stalagmites. She learns how to detect and mine gold, tungsten, and silver deposits. She makes thread from Claude's scales and weaves a beautiful dress to wear to meet the townspeople in, this time with neon colors.

Ten years pass, and as Sophia gets ready to climb up to meet the procession, she realizes that Claude hasn't directly told her the truth. She says, "Claude, you have told me many things, but I'm not sure you have told me the truth." Sophia had faced this test and stayed ten years, and she feels she deserves to know the truth.

He says, "You've always known the truth. It is inside you." Harking back to ancient times, Sophia had heard of the New Age, and she wondered whether this was an empty platitude. But it felt right.

She climbs up to meet the townsfolk, and she stands in her new dress, waiting at the edge of the precipice. She sees them coming toward her, laden with gifts for Claude and led by a young woman in a beautiful rainbow dress.

All of a sudden, someone sees Sophia and cries out, "It's Sophia! She's slain the dragon." As they come closer, Sophia quiets them down and explains that Claude meant them no harm. Half the townsfolk believe her and put her on their shoulders, carrying her back to town as a heroine. But the other half think that Sophia has lied and has hidden for ten years.

Sophia's notoriety soon recedes, and she goes back to being a bookbinder's daughter, escaping to the wilderness whenever she can and spying on the old ladies gossiping in the café. One day, she hears them talking about all the young men and boys in town, and when they get to her, they say, "That Sophia, that Sophia, she found the truth."

Sophia had many helpers to aid her in navigating the tests in the story. Her name meant wisdom, which I had inadvertently come up with This seemed perfect to me, because I was trying to transmit Earth's wisdom through the story. My idea was that one could find empowerment in the unconscious and heal the body through imagery.

Besides the symbology of her name, Sophia's helpers were her own characteristics, which included bravery and boldness. She was physically fit from her hikes in the wilderness. In addition, she had help from the town council, which gave her the opportunity to meet Claude. And of course, the dragon gave her an invitation to explore the caves of Earth. This, in turn, created an inner exploration of herself and the truth there.

Post-Traumatic Growth

The storytelling virtue of tests aligns with research findings in the field of Post-Traumatic Growth (PTG). Tests in stories are traumatic, sometimes even life-threatening, but certainly equivalent to the loss of a loved one or physical pain in real life. Richard Tedeschi and Lawrence Calhoun studied a phenomenon in which trauma can catalyze positive changes in some people. They isolated factors in people who grew emotionally after a trauma. Tedeschi notes that traumas challenge people's core beliefs. This sounds a lot like what characters face in stories, and possibly factors that help people grow after trauma are similar to the helpers that get the characters through the difficulties.

PTG can include positive psychological changes such as flourishing, positive emotions, thriving, coping emotions, positive reinterpretation, a sense of strength from adversity, and transformational coping. What seems to activate growth are rumination, self-disclosure, reduction of emotional distress, social support, and narrative development. This growth from trauma, according to Tedeschi, leads to wisdom.

Rumination is one factor prompting PTG. I like to reframe that as reflection. When people take a moment to reflect on a traumatic event, they can pause and wait for insight. People who experience growth after trauma can reflect on the trauma in a conscious manner, versus thoughts of the trauma spontaneously emerging. Another factor that prompts growth after a trauma is openness. Instead of staying in denial of the event, people are open to finding meaning. Openness and reflection/rumination are combined with an attitude of gratitude for the current state and forgiveness for the forces that created the trauma. From a storytelling perspective, PTG comes from accepting that trauma occurred and sensing the helpers that abound. Seeing and accepting social support is the key.

Other psychologists, such as B. L. Lancaster and J. T. Palframan, stress the importance of openness in coping with major life events. In their research, they looked at the transformative experiences of death: fear, feeling lost, feeling life is falling apart, feeling overloaded, or feeling that there is no way out. They identified the elements that helped with transformation such as letting go of beliefs, seeking trust, becoming self-aware, and realizing that there was support beyond the self. They write, "Continual movement into the unconscious, where the totality of the self is awakened, resulting in a reinterpretation of life purpose…radical reorganisation of one's identity, meaning and purpose of life."

The openness of the main character is a given in most stories. Sophia reflects throughout her story. In *The Children*, the villagers had to realize that they had abandoned the old woman when their children became sick. In *The Four Directions*, the people of the four directions had to accept their differences to overcome their jealousy and fear to share and communicate with other people. Of course, in *Ramayana*, Rama had to think long and hard before he accepted the situation that his younger brother would be the king, and then decide to go into the wilderness.

Stories illustrate the PTG characteristic of social support. A key for the main character to navigate tests in stories is the helpers, and one of the fundamentals of stories is that there are *always* helpers. This is the comforting aspect of stories that gives hope for the future—they teach that a person is never alone, and with adversity, help will come. In *Ramayana*, this is abundantly clear. Even though his father gave away the kingship, Rama knew his father still loved him.

Sita and Lakshmana went with Rama into the wilderness. After he helps the Monkey King defeat his enemy, the Monkey King's son, Hanuman the Flying Monkey-Man, helps Rama defeat Ravana. In *Keep on Steppin'*, oddly enough, Massa's children are helpers. By putting themselves out on a boat, they gave Dave the opportunity to act with natural compassion and Massa became indebted to him, eventually leading to his freedom. Also, Massa's scorn, manipulation, and cruelty toward Dave acted as reverse psychology. Dave was committed to do what he needed to do to be free.

Stories show that characters have the openness needed for PTG. Many stories showcase the character traits of the main character. Post-traumatic growth research points to one specific characteristic as related to healing—openness. Kwan Yin exemplified that characteristic repeatedly on her journey of tests. When she couldn't make money by weaving due to the famine, she was open to traveling to the Emperor's palace. When she met the Old Man in the mountains, she stopped her journey to give him water. When Lord Phoenix and Lord Tiger stole the sacred objects, she was open to the idea of keeping up her weaving amid threats of fire and even Khan's army. Her openness was rewarded with the magic of the dragon's robe she had made, which revealed the true identity of the Old Man, the Emperor himself.

Chapter Nine: The Virtue of Bravery

The third storytelling virtue is bravery. I place this in the west on the wheel, where it is metaphorically dusk, and people are being reflective. Bravery is a characteristic that many main characters rely on to master tests. Bravery sometimes comes as a surprise. Characters don't even know they are brave. They are just true to themselves, and bravery emerges.

Juan Bobo

Sometimes bravery comes from innocence. I return again to the story of Juan Bobo. He is a character from Puerto Rican culture who is a trickster or a fool. In his naiveté, he follows instructions literally, to the letter. In this version of *Juan Bobo*, he and his mother, a widow, lived in poverty. Juan was a good son, and he tried his best to do the right thing. But because he understood things in a literal fashion, sometimes it seemed as if what he did and said was silly, sometimes even offensive. This is why people call him Juan Bobo, "bobo" meaning fool.

One day, Juan's mother sent him to town to sell a fat chicken for money to buy rice and supplies. As he left the house, his mother said, "Be courteous and obedient."

A series of hilarious events unfolds. He comes across a procession with horses and a carriage. Juan Bobo bowed and said, "You have my deepest condolences." He said this because the only procession Juan had seen before was a funeral. The people in the wedding procession were outraged at what they perceived as an insult. The lead riders on horseback said, "No, no, you can't say that. It's insulting. You must say, 'Viva! Viva!'"

Ever obedient, Juan said, "Thanks very much."

Juan continues on his journey to the market, where he comes across a butcher and his three sons driving pigs. Juan, trying to do the right thing, says, "Viva! Viva!"

Juan frightened the pigs, and the pigs ran in all directions.

The butcher yelled at Juan, "You stupid boy, never say that! You scared the pigs. You need to say, "I hope God gives you two for each one.""

Ever courteous, Juan said, "Thank you very much. I will do just that."

Soon, Juan is nearer the market, and he sees a farmer who is burning weeds. Recalling his directions, Juan said, "I hope God gives you two for each one."

The farmer, incensed at this insult, claimed Juan should not say such a thing. He told Juan, "Who wants twice as many weeds? Don't say silly things. It is best if you help instead."

Ever obedient, Juan said, "Thank you very much. I will do exactly that." He feels horrible that he has made a mess of things, but he knows that he needs to keep on to the market to help his mother.

As he continues his journey, he comes across two men fighting, and of course he uses his last experience and tries to run toward them, saying, "Let me help you."

The men stopped fighting and started laughing. Juan was surprised they were not mad at him. However, the men told him to next time say, "Don't fight, señores." Dutifully, Juan tells them that he will do this. Juan finally gets to the market, sells the chicken, and buys some rice. He is finally pleased with himself as he heads home.

On the way home, Juan realized he was tired, so he climbed a tree to take a nap. After a bit, a storm came on, and rain started drizzling. As the water drops woke him, he heard a murmur of voices below him. Peeking through the leaves, he saw two thieves under the tree who had taken shelter from the rain.

The thieves were talking among themselves. One said, "Let's count the gold." The other one thought that they should wait, and the two got into a fistfight.

Juan, remembering the admonishments he had received, said, "Please don't fight, señores."

At that moment, the bag of rice that Juan was holding as he rested broke open and rained down on the thieves. One thief yelled, "Help, help, the God of the storm has discovered us. Run, run!"

Juan Bobo climbed down and saw that the space below the tree was deserted. The thieves were gone, but the gold remained. After the rain stopped, Juan picked up the gold and returned home. His mother asked, "Where is the rice?"

Juan said, "Here is some gold!" Feeling proud, he said, "It is easy to get rich if a person is courteous and obedient to everyone."

Juan may not seem to personify bravery, but he was brave in his innocence, speaking up to everyone he met. Sometimes innocence and naiveté result in bravery. In Juan's case, bravery came from being honest. Juan is polite and does as he was told. This may seem foolish, and certainly the name Juan Bobo implies that he is silly, possibly even laughable. But one quality he has is keeping to his virtues, regardless of whatever is happening around him. In his innocence, he is brave, and, paradoxically, he is empowered because he does not act based on social norms or expectations.

Lilith

Sometimes bravery comes from speaking out. Lilith was brave when standing up to patriarchal power and masculine domination. Even though the "Me Too" movement against misogyny began in 2020, Lilith was fighting it as far back as 4200 BCE. The first reference to her name is as a Mesopotamian goddess. She later appears in 800 BCE as Adam's first wife. The story goes that God threw her out of Eden because she didn't want to be under Adam all the time during sex. The story continues that she came back as a serpent tempting Eve. She not only spoke up to God but also brought knowledge to humankind. The stories I've found end there, so there isn't any information about the consequences of Lilith breaking up God's plan for the human race.

In some Jewish communities, Lilith is the monster who will steal children after dark, and parents remind children to stay home and avoid Lilith. She might be compared to La Llorona, a heroine or demon of Latin American folktales. The *La Llorona* story is a bit different but has the same element of standing up to patriarchy.

La Llorona

La Llorona, an indigenous Mexican, married a handsome conquistador, and they had two sons. She lived with him in a ranchero, and they were seemingly very happy. However, one day when she was on an errand in the village, she saw him with a beautiful, young Spanish woman, the daughter of the Spanish governor. He was holding the young woman's hand, and she learned through her relatives in the village that he planned to marry her, abandon La Llorona, and take their sons to live with his new wife. She realized he planned to pretend that their marriage never existed.

Distraught, betrayed, and mad with grief, La Llorona takes their sons to the river and drowns them in a fit of rage. She does it to hurt her husband. Coming to her senses, she wails and rends her clothes. Then every night, she goes to the river, driven to psychosis. She wails and wails. At night, you can hear La Llorona—the weeping woman—wailing in the river for her sons. Parents tell their children not to go out by the river at night, just like Lilith, using an archetype of a woman dominated by men to scare children.

Some feminists have rehabilitated both Lilith and La Llorona. For example, there is a Jewish feminist literary journal titled *Lilith* that celebrates Lilith as a liberator of women. After all, in the stories, Lilith stood up to both God and Adam, and this brought knowledge to the human race. Feminist scholars see Lilith as empowered, not evil. Misogyny and patriarchy blame women for many problems that occur. Lilith acted as a powerful feminine archetype, refusing to go along with a system of control.

Similarly, Latina feminists have written about La Llorona in a revisionist way, removing her from the evil category. In Mexican stories, La Llorona is called Maria. When the Spanish colonists invaded Mexico and what is now Arizona, New Mexico, and California, young indigenous girls were raped and made mistresses of Spanish conquistadors. La Llorona's actions were indefensible. But it could have been that La Llorona had been raped by a conquistador as a young girl of thirteen. He had used her and made promises. So even though drowning her sons was a horrific and unforgivable action, one can see the sexual abuse of a young preteen girl in perhaps a different light.

As noted earlier, my non-profit, the WHEEL Council, held conferences for several years. The conferences were named Storytelling Teaches, Storytelling Heals. A women's drama group from Tucson, Arizona, did performance art by acting out the story of La Llorona in 1995. I was astounded by the performance. They represented La Llorona as an empowered feminist figure who was acting out to protest rape and the oppression of indigenous people. I take no position. But I think the women in stories are often marginalized and shown as whores or angels, never a balanced, integrated vision of women. Possibly the truth is in between.

Isis

I return to the story of Isis to detail how she embodies bravery. Isis shows up in the historical annals around 2500 BCE. She was one of the quadruplets, along with Seth, Osiris, and Nephthys. There are many different stories about these quads. But all support the fact that Isis became the Queen of the Nile.

There is one story that Isis found her power by stalking the sun god Re. At that time in this story, no one knew the name of the sun god. But all knew that if one found out his name, that person would have power. Isis stalked the sun god every day and watched from the east to the west as he made his transit across the earth. As the sun god became old, he couldn't quite control his spittle. His spittle fell out of his mouth one day, and Isis found it and made a snake from it.

At his next rotation, the snake bit the sun god. He yelled in pain, and Isis told the sun god she would help him if he told her his name. The sun god tried many false names. But Isis was not fooled. One storytelling lesson is that the main character bodes no fools and can source out the truth. Finally, the sun god told Isis his name, Re, and Isis was imbued with the power of the sun.

She used that power to find her husband Osiris after her brother Seth had killed him. She and her sister Nephthys flew out of their temple to fly over the Nile. They found Osiris on a sandbank. Isis mated with his dead body. Out of this, Horus was born, and he became a great Pharaoh of Egypt, possibly foretelling the story of an immaculate birth.

These ancient stories defy logical interpretation. The stories contain fantastic elements. There are rarely quadruplets, and in modern times, they don't marry each other. Women don't have wings or mate with their dead husbands. But all this happens in Isis's story. The story is complex and has many interpretations. But I think bravery is Isis's main characteristic. Isis is the Empress of Egypt and the Nile. She represents the regenerative nature of the Nile. Each season, the river dries up and then it floods, bringing water to crops to sustain life. Isis is brave as she takes flight to find Osiris. She is undaunted to keep her royal hereditary line alive. She mates with her dead husband to bring forth another ruler, Horus. The ankh symbol is a representation of the power that Isis forged with her bravery.

Gaia

As previously mentioned, the story of the Greek earth goddess Gaia has many lessons. Gaia's story shows how sometimes bravery comes from being smart. Gaia is the ancient Greek goddess of Earth. Her name is derived from the root words for Earth and grandmother. Her story conveys that she created the sea, mountains, and skies.

Gaia's mate was Ouranos, and they birthed the twelve Titans and the one-eyed Cyclops. Ouranos hated the Cyclops and wanted to destroy them. Gaia could not abide the destruction of life, and she enlisted their son, Cronos, to stop Ouranos from eating the Cyclops. The next time Ouranos came amorously to Gaia, Cronos cut off his genitals and threw them into the sea. Thus, Aphrodite was born. Ouranos was banished to the sky. Even though the Cyclops were ugly monsters, Gaia still protected them. I think this story shows that sometimes, to be brave, a person, and in this case also a goddess, needs to ask for help. Gaia asked Cronos, her son, for help.

Gaia's story demonstrates another example of her bravery to protect life. Cronos was set to take over his father's position, but there was a prophecy that Cronos's son, Zeus, would one day take over. Cronos was set on destroying Zeus so that he could stay in power. Gaia tricked Cronos into swallowing a stone instead of swallowing Zeus. The rest is history, so to speak. Most people know Zeus as the ruler of all the gods of Mount Olympus.

As with other non-rational, ancient stories, this one is a little difficult to make sense of. One could see Gaia as being duplicitous, tricking Cronos to eat a stone or getting Cronos to wound Ouranos. But in both cases, she used her wits to find a way to protect life. After all, she is the goddess mother of Earth.

Buffalo Woman

I return to the story in more detail *Buffalo Woman* illustrate the virtue of bravery. Buffalo Woman's husband shows bravery by taking risks. In this Osage story, there was a young hunter who was very good at his job. From his Native American heritage and values, he was very respectful of the buffalo spirit. He only shot what he needed and thanked the buffalo spirit after a kill. He and his family were careful to use all the buffalo for their daily and tribal needs. For example, the skin was used for clothes, the meat was dried for the winter food supply, and the bones were fashioned as weapons and ceremonial objects.

One time, while on a hunt, the hunter noticed a beautiful young woman by a stream. He'd never seen her before. Her hair fell down over her shoulders, unlike the women of his tribe who always kept their hair braided. He moved near her and smelled wild sage and prairie flowers. He fell madly in love instantly.

The story doesn't tell what ensued then, but jumps to the time when the hunter and the maiden are married. It turns out she comes from the Buffalo Nation. They have a child whom they named Calf Boy. The hunter's family did not like her, as she was not from their tribe. When the hunter was gone on a hunting trip, his family came and told her she should leave, saying the hunter didn't really love her. This cruelty added to the fact that she missed her buffalo family.

One day, she took Calf Boy and ran from the village. The hunter saw them leave and tracked them. After a long day, he saw smoke from a campfire and found them. Calf Boy welcomed his father and said his mother had made a meal for him. After the meal, Buffalo Woman said that he should go home. She was leaving because his people were cruel. She exhorted him not to follow, saying it was very dangerous. The hunter said, "I love you, and I will go wherever you go."

The next morning, when he got up, his wife and son were gone, already having broken down the tipi. The hunter tracked them all day and finally found them. Calf Boy ran out and told him his mother had said he shouldn't follow them. The hunter said, "I love you, and I will go wherever you go." That night, he slept with his wife and tied her to him, wrapping her hair around his wrist. But this was to no avail. Again in the morning, the hunter saw the tipi gone, as was his wife and son. He followed their tracks again, but at a certain point, the tracks turned from human to buffalo. From the top of a ridge, the hunter saw a great herd of buffalo in the plains below. A young buffalo ran up the ridge to the hunter. It turned out to be Calf Boy.

Calf Boy said, "Father, go back. The herd will kill you."

The hunter said, "No, I will never go back."

Calf Boy said, "Stay if you insist, but listen to me, whatever happens, do not show you are afraid. They will want you to show that you understand the Buffalo Nation by picking my mother out of the herd. I will flick my ear, and I'll put a cocklebur on mother's back."

Just then, a huge bull came charging toward them. He was named Chief Bull. It sounded like thunder as his hooves hit the ground in front of the hunter. Minding what Calf Boy said, the hunter showed no fear. Chief Bull was impressed and said, "You have saved yourself with your courage. You have a strong heart. Straight-up Person, follow me."

The buffalo herd parted. Chief Bull and the hunter, now named Straight-Up Person, came down and walked through the herd. As they neared the middle of the herd, there was a painted tipi. The herd formed a large circle around Straight-Up Person and Chief Bull.

Chief Bull said, "Now you must find your wife, Buffalo Woman, and your son, Calf Boy."

Luckily, Straight-Up Person was able to use the clues his son had given him, and he found his family. Chief Bull was impressed, and he said, "Straight-Up Person showed he was willing to die for his family. We will make him one of us."

Chief Bull took the man into the tipi and covered him with a buffalo skin. For three days and three nights, the buffalo moved around the tipi in a circle, eventually knocking it down. They rolled over the hunter again and again until all the breath was pushed out of him. Then they breathed new life into him. He stood up again as a buffalo. His bravery forged new bonds between his tribe and the buffalo. The tribe sang the praises of the buffalo, and the buffalo provided food and warm skins in the winter for the tribe. The hunter risked his life for the love of his wife and son. There is no greater bravery than that.

Chapter Ten: The Virtue of Beauty

Stories as metaphors for life showcase how normal life can change suddenly and dramatically as tests present themselves. The job of story characters, or everyday people, is to see the obvious or hidden helpers to face, survive, and even vanquish adversity. This creates a transformation in heroes and heroines and even regular folks to create a new normal. One profound helper in stories is noticing beauty within and without. Seeing beauty, celebrating beauty, and allowing beauty to touch one's life sustains one through the tests one experiences. Noticing beauty creates awe, appreciation, and gratitude for life—antidotes to the difficulties of navigating stress.

Ganesha

Beauty comes in different forms, and in the story *Ganesha*, beauty comes in the beneficence that Ganesha bestows. I return to his story to showcase the role of beauty. Recall that Ganesha was Shiva's son whose head was replaced with an elephant's after Shiva ripped it off. He is part man and part elephant and a major deity in India. When I worked in India as a Fulbright scholar teaching graduate studies, I kept a postcard of Ganesha in my wallet. This was in 1992, and I had been doing yoga long before, attending the Iyengar Institute in San Francisco since 1980. As a result, I was immersed in Hindu philosophy and had been attracted to Ganesha's story. I remember listening to NPR while driving from Prescott, Arizona, to Palos Verdes, California, to visit my brother. The show featured a storyteller narrating Ganesha's story. I knew he was an archetype who removed obstacles and brought "beneficence," a word defined as doing good. I also associate beneficence with beauty—doing good to me is the ultimate beauty.

The Fulbright organization, as part of the U.S. Department of State, oriented me and the other professors about living in India. We were exhorted with all sorts of advice about how to stay safe and how to keep our valuables secure. Because of my knowledge of Ganesha's story, I placed a postcard in my wallet to bring beneficence to my trip and keep pickpockets away. Based on the Fulbright information, I knew pickpocketing might be a risk in New Delhi, as it is in any big city. I lived in a little town in Northern Arizona. I bought a postcard of Ganesha at a New Age bookstore and put it in my fanny pack. When the crowds surrounded me while getting off a train in New Delhi, I knew I had Ganesha in my pocket.

During my time there, we had some problems finding basic services. As a member of the U.S. individualistic society, what anthropologists call a low-context culture, it was hard for me to adapt to a communitarian culture where one needed to get things done through other people. I was working in a very small town, Vallabh Vidyanagar, in the state of Gujarat. My family was with me: my two children, and my husband. Being a closet Marxist, it was hard for me to hire bearers, cooks, and drivers to make life easy. When I went to a street seller of vegetables, a man would say to me, "Where is your bearer?" One had to work with other people to get things done. If I went to the bank by myself, no one would talk to me. But if I took a driver who did the talking, it worked. Needless to say, it was a learning curve for me, and Ganesha gave me confidence.

In addition, maybe it was my imagination, but I think I had visions of Ganesha. Psychic phenomena were alive and well in our remote corner of India. One night, I was asleep when I suddenly woke up and saw Ganesha floating in a corner. He was floating on air, all shiny and golden. Ram Dass said Hinduism was gaudy. The postcard I had of Ganesha might be seen as gaudy—bright colors of red and yellow, and many sparkly necklaces. His statues were also somewhat gaudy. Statues are adorned with flowers and jewels. Sometimes he is seated on a large gold throne. In this case, the decorations symbolize all kinds of riches—physical, emotional, and spiritual.

I learned to rely on his beneficence to get food for our family. We were on a campus that the Swiss had created for an agriculture institute. But my teaching assignment was several miles away. I needed to take a rickshaw to go teach, and my two children, ages thirteen and fifteen, were stuck at the agricultural studies campus. We learned to walk or find a bicycle to go to the local store, which was quite small. It was almost a storefront. There were crowds of people there, and one had to yell to get noticed for milk and eggs. There was a cart nearby with fresh vegetables, peppers, potatoes, and tomatoes. We managed. I learned to go to the nearby street to get plastic bags of water buffalo milk in the mornings. So we survived, and my children lost weight, but they learned to value the basics of having food. They grew up in middle-class America, and this experience put their heads on the right track for gratitude and appreciation of material bounty. Sometimes I looked at the postcard and asked Ganesha for food, and our neighbors invited us to dinner. It was so hard to learn the culture, even after months. I had been told not to say thank you to people, as it was insulting. Of course, people would help you; it was expected. I ended up buying cakes for my neighbors as a thank-you. It showed me I hadn't quite learned the culture.

With the postcard in my passport bag, I was never ripped off, even in downtown New Delhi, where people surrounded me with their hands out. I was a big fan of Ganesha. Beneficence populates beauty. Beauty might be a woman with pleasing facial features or a gorgeous, toned, muscular body. We might think of paintings, sculptures, or arresting architectural buildings that exude beauty. But with Ganesha, I think beauty might be seen through a different lens. Beauty is having our basic human needs met. Beauty for Ganesha is being willing to lose one's head, accept the reality of one's life, and trust that our needs will be provided.

The White Spider

The Uruguayan story of *The White Spider* is a great ode to beauty. This story is about love across social classes and the fact that the beauty of nature bridges that gap. Piki is a poor but noble young man who is in love with Taukira, the Chieftain's daughter. They meet by happenstance. While Piki was walking to a stream through the forest near his house, Taukira pulled up in a canoe at the same place.

There are many elements of beauty in this story. There is the beauty of the forest. There is the beauty of a Chieftain's daughter, Taukira. The White Spider is Piki's friend who lives in a shrub near Piki's home. The White Spider is beautiful, and the gift the spider weaves, a lace shawl, is beautiful. It is a gift for Piki to give to Taukira. There is also the beauty of Piki's humility. They fell in love, but her father would not let her marry a poor man. Taukira accepts his position. Piki gives up his aspirations to win Taukira's hand, but his mother exhorts him to have faith. Afterward, when he goes to the stream to get water, the White Spider miraculously talks to him. All these elements of beauty help Piki and Taukira overcome their struggles due to their different social classes and gain the Chieftain's acceptance, so they can unite in love.

That's the basic summary of the story, but let's look at it closer, starting with Piki. He is poor yet strong. He knows the rainforest around his home, and he often makes forays there. He loves the greens, the smells, the animal noises, and the bird calls of the rainforest. Once, during the predawn, when a few rays of light drifted into his dwelling, he was awakened by the din of birds echoing under the dense leaf canopy. He noticed the wildlife, the birds, the rodents, and even the spiders. He walked to the spring for water, and as he crouched to fill the earthen jar, he noticed something sparkling like the sun. Under the yerba mate bush was a spider's web. He sees the tiny white spider sitting in the web. The wind came up, and the spider dropped into the spring. Piki scooped her up and held her in the sunlight until she was dry. He placed her carefully on a rock near the web. He saw her crawl back onto her web.

Piki and his mother lived near a stream, and on another morning, they both heard paddles splash. Piki ran to the stream and saw a beautiful young woman in a canoe. She wore a white cotton tunic with a purple sash. Her hair was ebony, and she had lavender orchids in her braids. At a given moment, they both saw each other, and there was an instant connection. After that day, the young woman took solitary walks in the forest to pass by Piki's place. They started to run into each other most days, seemingly by chance. Piki found out her name by asking his mother, who said, "She is Taukira, the Chieftain's daughter and has been away at her mother's village for a time. But now she is back."

As the two young people met in the forest, they shared berries and began to fall in love. The village people noticed their meetings and were happy that these two fine young people might wed. However, the Chieftain had other ideas and wanted Taukira to marry the strongest suitor. He set up many tests of racing, swimming, and hunting. Piki won many, but then the Chieftain changed his mind and created a new test. He said, "The young man who brings Taukira the most beautiful gift will win her hand."

Piki was distraught. Since he was poor, he could not buy a beautiful gift. He had no hope. But his mother said to him, "Have faith. You will know what to do." Piki shared his fears with Taukira, but Taukira was confident that Piki would win. Young men from surrounding villages brought skins of panthers, gold jewelry, and parrots with gorgeous feathers of green, turquoise, red, and blue. Piki was worried, but both his mother and Taukira told him to have courage.

Piki knew he must have a very special gift for Taukira if he was to win her. He hiked to the special place by the stream where he saw the White Spider. He was distraught, but all of a sudden, he heard a voice: "I'm here in the bush. I can help you." Confused, Piki looked around, but then he heard. "I'm here in the bush. I'm your White Spider, and I can help you win the Princess." Looking into the bush, Pika saw the tiny white weaver moving feverishly. He knew to leave the spider alone at that point, and he ran home with hope in his heart.

Piki returned to the spring at dawn, the time when the monkeys and parrots screamed. He looked for the spider in the yerba mate bush, but alas, there was no spider. After looking again, he saw a beautiful shawl with images of guava flowers, orchids, and begonias. The beauty of the shawl was magnificent. He ran and gave it to the Chieftain. Through the White Spider's beautiful weaving, he had won his beautiful Taukira.

The beauty in this story comes from nature: Piki's connection to the forest, the river, the springs, and the subtle beauty of a White

Spider. The story shows that beauty is not in material riches but in the riches of nature.

Coyote and His Pups

As I worked with Native American tribes in Arizona, I learned the power of storytelling to convey wisdom from knowledge beyond the rational. Even though some stories didn't seem logical or rational, there is meaning. Stories go from the heart of the storyteller to the heart of the listener. There is an emotional content to stories that communicates with the heart-mind-body.

I knew this from my experience as a little girl listening to stories on TV. I used to watch a show called *Romper Room*. In the show, there was a kindly, mother-like figure sitting on a little chair. After reading a story from a huge book, she held a huge magnifying glass, saying, "I see Mary. I see Tommy." I listened every day, waiting for her to see me. One day she said, "I see Annabelle," and I was thrilled. This *Romper Room* lady also said after reading a story, "And the moral of this story is…." I think in Western tradition, using logic to understand stories is the norm. However, in other cultures, there is a knowing beyond logic. Wisdom is going beyond, or transrational. To understand these stories, one can't really answer the *Romper Room* lady. The moral of the story is not clear. One listens to and appreciates the story, allowing the meaning to sink in. Then awareness and insight come.

What I found in listening to and reading Native American stories is that the stories weren't the same as in European fairytales. For example, for the Southwest tribes in the U.S., stories about Coyote are very important. Coyote may not be a logical choice for a hero or as a lead character. He might not even seem like an anti-hero. He is a laughable archetype of human vulnerability, fragility, and resilience. Listeners can identify with his mistakes and smile, even laugh. After his screw-ups, he still ends up on his feet. He perseveres and continues on to more adventures. Coyote helps listeners know that making mistakes and bouncing back is part of the human condition. The cartoon character Wile E. Coyote in *The Road Runner Show* is a good example of this. It is really not possible at the end to say, "And the moral of this story is…."

For example, in one Coyote story I heard, Coyote thought he was catching quail to roast for dinner. But the quails tricked him. They perched on Coyote's backside, and he dug out part of his own rump, thinking it was the quails. He roasted his rump and was proud of himself for getting the quails. Gee, one might ask what the moral of this story is. Coyote was fooled by the quails, but he was still alive. Coyote's stories help listeners laugh at Coyote's failings but also laugh at themselves and others who experience making mistakes or being foolish.

I noticed a difference between the patterns of Native American and European stories. In European fairytales, the number three recurs. But in American Indian tales, the number four recurs. For me, this was resonant with my research on wheels, where the number four, as in the four cardinal directions, is important. Also, I noticed that there was not always a clear end to a story with a logical moral. The endings are less final as well. Something happens, but it is not clear what the meaning is. The intuitive mind needs to come out and play to understand the significance of the story.

After reading and hearing Coyote stories, I decided to make one up myself. I wanted it to be an oral story. I never wrote anything down since I wanted to merge with the oral tradition. As I mentioned earlier, one of my Tohono O'odham friends said to me, "You think knowledge comes from a book. We think it comes from elders." Since my psychological studies were about imagery, I visualized the story as I told it to make sure I was using vivid language. I write the story here to share.

My story goes like this. Coyote got up in the morning and crawled out of the cave while his pups were still sleeping. He felt great about himself. His chest was puffed out, and he strutted back and forth. He had made a kill the night before and brought his family meat. His strutting back and forth on the rock ledge outside of the cage had awakened his pups, and they ran out and clamored all over Coyote. Jumping on his back, they cried. "Daddy, Daddy, come play with us."

Coyote said, "Not now, pups. I'm too busy thinking about myself."

Coyote heard a screech in the sky and saw a bird with a perfectly chiseled white alabaster tail and a white head. He looked up and saw Eagle. As Coyote looked back at his own tail, it seemed sloppy and mangy. He said, "I wish I had Eagle's tail."

The pups came out again to ask their daddy to play with them: "Daddy, Daddy, come play with us."

But Coyote had the same response: "Not now, pups. I'm too busy thinking about myself."

Coyote felt his chest fall a little lower, and his strut was a little dampened.

It was getting on to noon, and the sun was high in the sky. Coyote heard another animal crashing through the underbrush toward the stream directly below his rock ledge. As he was sitting on the stone ledge, Coyote saw Bear's gigantic paws hitting the sand by the stream's beach as Bear prepared to fish for salmon there. The prints were huge, and the claws sunk into the sand. Coyote looked down at his own paws and said, "I wish I had Bear's paws."

Again, the pups came out asking for Coyote to play with them. Again Coyote put them off since he was thinking about the tail and the paws he wanted.

"Daddy, Daddy, come play with us," begged the pups.

Coyote said, "Not now, pups. I'm too busy thinking about myself."

Now Coyote was sitting on the stone ledge, no longer walking back and forth, and his chest was almost caved in.

As the day passed and the evening unfolded, Coyote heard a splash in the stream. He looked down and saw an animal cavorting and swimming on his back. When the swimmer turned over, Coyote noticed his beautiful coat. It glistened as it shed water. It was Beaver. Coyote looked at his own back, with its variegated colors of brown, and it seemed almost shaggy. "I wish I had Beaver's fur."

The pups came out again: "Daddy, Daddy, come play with us."

Coyote said, "Not now, pups. I'm too busy thinking about myself."

The pups were getting tired of asking Coyote to play. They sulked back to the cave. Totally dejected, Coyote lay flat on what was now a cold slab of granite. The pups went to sleep, and Coyote kept saying, "I wish I had Eagle's tail. I wish I had Bear's paws. And I really, really wish I had Beaver's fur."

Soon it was night, and the Milky Way was a brilliant streak across the sky. Coyote heard a flap of wings, and in a whoosh, a bird landed on a snag near the granite outcropping. It was Owl.

Owl said, "Silly Coyote, what are you doing out here on a cold granite ledge? I heard you say you want Eagle's tail, Beaver's fur, and Bear's paws. Coyote, we need you to be you. You are the smartest of all of us. You can go in and out of the human places to find food. You are right just the way you are."

But Coyote ignored Owl, and he stayed awake all night thinking of himself and who he wanted to be. Animal brothers and sisters walking nearby could hear him say all night long, "I wish I had Eagle's tail. I wish I had Bear's paws. And I really, really wish I had Beaver's fur."

As noted previously, the point of stories isn't always about "and the moral is…." Some stories are told to prompt listeners to allow the images, characters, and actions soak in. As mentioned earlier, Terry Tafoya, storyteller from a Northwest Indian Tribe, says that stories plant symbols in the mind, and over time, these symbols grow and become important. I think this story about Coyote for me is about settling into one's own being and becoming comfortable with it. Often, people feel bad about who they are and want to be someone different. "Silly humans," Owl might say. He might also say, "Settle into who you are. You are the perfect version of yourself." My Coyote story is about the individual beauty of each element of creation. It is about the beauty of self-acceptance.

Chapter Eleven: The Virtue of Death and Rebirth

"The hero-heroine is a continuous shattering of the crystallizations of the moment…[the] passage of the magical threshold is a transit into a sphere of rebirth."
-Joseph Campbell

According to Campbell, heroes undergo a process of self-annihilation and a metamorphosis as they survive a series of trials. "Self-annihilation" is a strong word that conveys the seriousness of the life journey. Many writers and spiritual teachers seem to gloss over the difficulty of life, indicating that people can get what they want. But the truth is revealed in stories—that difficulty, pain, and death can happen in life. Also, Western civilization seems to deny the eventuality of death. Accepting death as a part of life comes from the wisdom of stories. Sometimes, out of a metaphoric death comes rebirth, a new perspective on life. Sometimes, out of the reality of death comes the wisdom of a life well lived, helping others. Death and rebirth in stories is a theme showing how heroes and heroines take mortal risks to face death to help others.

John the True

Death is present in *John the True*. During the earlier discussion about the tests in the storytelling cycle, I conveyed that John was willing to face death to save his King and future.

Recall in the story that the King recently inherited his birthright following his father's death. The new King had been away fighting battles. On returning to his castle, the King's best friend since childhood, John, and the King decided to explore the castle. They ran from room to room in the enormous castle, exploring its contents. Finally, they came to a room full of furniture and old paintings. The King looked up at a painting on the wall and stopped cold.

"What are you staring at, my King? You look like you have seen a ghost," yelled John to get the King's attention.

The King, startled, looked at John: "Who is she? Who is that beautiful Princess with skin as white as snow, cheeks as red as blood, and hair as black as ebony? She is the most beautiful woman I have ever seen. You must find her for me," the King yelled, looking like a wild man. His eyes were as big as saucers, and his hair stood on end as if he had been hit by lightning.

"Calm down," John said. "This is the Princess of the Golden Horde. Your father has been at war with her father for the past twenty years. In fact, you've been fighting her father's army. You could never marry her. Turn that picture around and face it to the wall," John said as he patted the King on the shoulder. Then he took the painting off the wall and turned it.

Days passed, and the King could not think of anything but the Princess. He tried to forget her, but he grew listless, stopped eating, and would not get out of his bed.

John could not stand watching his King suffer, so he went to him and said, "Be of good cheer, my King. I will go get her for you."

"But how can you do that? You told me that we were enemies and that I could never have her. I have decided to die. I am starving myself, since I cannot live without her," the King claimed as he sucked in his cheeks to look as if he was starving.

"I can't stand to see you this way, and I have an idea. Give me a ship and load it with furniture made of gold," said John. So the King did what was asked. John was a tricky guy, and he knew the way to a Princess's heart. He sailed to the port of the Empire of the Golden Horde, but he did not let on that he was from the kingdom of the Horde's hated enemies. He pretended he was a merchant on his way to another kingdom with a tribute for the King there. He had stopped at the Horde to pick up the supplies. Rumors had reached the King, Queen, and their beautiful daughter (with skin as white as snow, cheeks as red as blood, and hair as black as ebony) about the ship containing furniture made of gold. One night, the royal family came down to the dock to see the furniture. John the True invited them over the gangway into the ship and onto the deck, where the gold furniture was displayed. The Princess fell in love with a dressing table made of gold with crystal mirrors.

"Father, I must have this. Look how beautiful I am in this mirror. Make him sell this to you," the Princess pleaded.

"No, this is not for sale. It is for a special purpose, and I am not allowed to tell who it is for," John said stoically.

That night, the Princess came down with her maid to persuade John to sell the dressing table. As John saw her board the boat, he ran to the captain and told him to set sail as soon as the Princess went into the cabin.

"Please, please, Master John, will you sell me this dressing table? I will give you more gold than it is worth," the Princess said, standing regally and ready to command John to do her bidding.

"Well, it is this way. I have been told to find a very special woman. One whose skin is as white as snow, whose cheeks are as red as blood, and whose hair is as black as ebony. Only then can I give the table to her," claimed John as he looked out at the water, watching the Princess carefully from the corner of his eye to see how she was reacting.

"Let's go into the cabin, and I will show you my reflection in the mirror," the Princess explained emphatically. "I am that woman. You will see. I have snow white skin, red blood cheeks, and black ebony hair. You must give this to me."

At that, she ran below deck. As John followed her, the ship set sail. In a little while, the Princess felt the motion of the ship as it rocked on the waves.

"What is happening? What? What? You've kidnapped me!" the Princess shrieked.

"Wait, my Princess. You must listen for a bit, and then I will take you back if you want," John said, and the Princess calmed down. "My King has fallen in love with you, and he is such a wonderful man. He is now ill with sickness since he cannot have you. Please come back to meet him, and then decide whether you can marry him," John explained.

The Princess eyed the dressing table and the other gold furniture and decided to check this out. They went on their voyage for over a month. On one long, sunny day, the Princess was resting on the deck watching the birds fly by. She noticed three Ravens flying overhead. She heard them cawing. John, standing nearby, was a huntsman and could understand bird language.

The Ravens seemed to portend death: "Caw! Caw! There is the Princess. She thinks that she will go to the King and be married, but it will not happen," crowed the first Raven.

"Why not?" asked John.

"Well, when she first meets the King, he will put her on his horse. But it is a wild horse, and they will both be thrown off and die," the Raven continued.

"But can't this be prevented?" John asked.

"Only if someone cuts off the horse's head. But if he tells anyone why he did it, he will turn to stone up to his knees," the Raven warned.

John seemed to be wise of the way of the animals and their prophecies, so he listened to them carefully to stave off the death of his King.

"Caw! Caw! There is another danger. When the King drinks wine at his wedding feast, he will die because it will be poisoned. The only way to stop it is to throw the goblet from his mouth. But if the person who does this tells anyone, he will turn to stone up to his heart," explained the second Raven.

"Caw! Caw! There is still another danger. On their wedding night, a dragon will come into the bridal bedroom and kill both the King and the Princess. Someone must drive off the dragon, but if he tells anyone, he will turn to stone from head to toe," called the third Raven.

The Ravens flew off. John was deeply troubled and decided he must save his King, even if it meant becoming a stone statue. John faced the reality of his situation and what was needed to save the King and the soon-to-be Queen.

It came to pass just as the first Raven had said. When the Princess arrived on shore, she immediately fell in love with the King. He reached down to put the Princess on his horse. Just as he did this,

John rushed forward and cut off the horse's head. The King's guards tried to arrest John, but the King would not let them.

"Stop, this is my dear friend. He must have had some reason," the King proclaimed.

Then the second Raven's prophecy was fulfilled. At the wedding dinner, the King brought a goblet to his lips, and John leapt to strike the cup to the ground. Again, the King's guards tried to arrest him, and again, the King would not let them.

"Stop, this is my dear friend. He must have had some reason," the King decried again.

Finally, the third Raven's prophecy was realized. Immediately after dinner, John walked quietly up the steps from the dining hall to the royal bedroom. He gently opened the door and saw the dragon waiting just inside the window, hidden by a curtain. He moved quickly to the curtain, drawing his sword and striking at the dragon's heart. The dragon moved too quickly, and John did not kill it. However, the dragon was gravely wounded, and he jumped from the window to fly away to his cave to die. John turned around toward the door with the sword in his hand, dripping blood.

"John, what have you done? This is too much. I can't trust you after this. Guards, take him. He will be executed tomorrow," the King cried, distraught to have to kill his foster brother.

Bowing on one knee with his head bent, John said, "Do you want me to explain all this?"

"Yes, of course, my dear foster brother. Help me make sense of this," the King reached down and pulled up John.

As John began to explain, his feet turned to stone. As he explained more, he turned to stone up to his heart. Then, as he explained about the dragon, he turned to stone up through his head. His mouth was still open as he froze to stone, speaking his last word.

The King and Queen placed John the True, now a statue, in the courtyard in the plaza outside the palace. They had twin boys, and as the boys grew, the King and Queen told them how John had saved their lives. The boys would march by the statue and salute John the True. Then one night, the Queen had a dream that if she would scrape the dragon's blood off the floor of the bedroom and put it on the statue, then John the True would become a man again. She did just that, and the King's foster brother was restored to life.

Death and rebirth are strong themes in this story. The Ravens had predicted the future and told John how to prevent threats to the King and Queen's lives. But one Raven also explained that if John said why he was doing this, then John would turn to stone. He had to do things such as killing a horse before the King's betrothed mounted it, knocking a goblet out of the King's hand, and slaying a dragon in the bridal bedroom. So John did these things, and he faced his death because of his loyalty to and love for the King. Eventually, John had turned to stone because he had to confess to the King. The story is a tale of death and rebirth in which rebirth comes from loyalty and true action.

It is an odd story. Not many people would actually die to protect a friend as John the True did. There are uncomfortable aspects of the story, as John the True tricked the potential Queen into sailing back to the King's kingdom. But the story's theme is staying true to one's values. In this case, it was John's commitment to his King, loyalty, and love. Also, the Queen's trust in her intuition revealed how to restore John in a dream. Love for another and trust in one's intuition are helpers in facing death and rebirth.

Deirdre

The Celtic story of *Deirdre* has a prominent theme of death as a consequence of love. It does not have a happy ending, but sometimes rebirth is metaphoric, not a physical reality. Rather, in the celebration of life, the hero and heroine inspire others.

In this story, a Chieftain has a beautiful baby girl named Deirdre. When a druid saw the beautiful child, he prophesied she would be the most beautiful woman in the kingdom, but she would be the death of two kings. Her father decided to hide her in the woods to protect her and others. She lived with the poetess Leabharcham. One day, King Conchobhar was riding through the woods, and after seeing Dierdre, he immediately fell in love. He made her promise to marry him when she came of age.

Deirdre grew up and became more and more beautiful. Living in the woods, she loved nature and learned to talk to the ravens and foxes. When she was almost at maidenhood, she was out gathering flowers. She saw a truly handsome man with jet black hair approaching. They immediately fell in love. She later learned his name, Naoise, and he had two younger brothers, Ainlé and Ardán. The poetess loved Dierdre and wanted her to be happy. She arranged a meeting for Deirdre and Naoise. Their love was sealed. Everyone knew that Deirdre was promised to King Conchobhar and that he would not relinquish his claim on Deirdre without a fight. Deirdre and Naoise, with his brothers, fled to Alba, then ancient Scotland. They found a beautiful spot on a stream where fish were so abundant that they jumped right into their nets.

King Conchobhar learned of this and planned his revenge. He had his trusted knight, Fergus, whom Naoise and his brothers also trusted, call them back to Ireland for the massing of his knights. They couldn't refuse. Fergus assured Naoise and his brothers that they would be protected. But on the way back to Ireland, King Conchobhar had his druid call down curses on Deirdre and the brothers. First, he sent a great wave, and Ainlé drowned while the others swam through. Then he made the ground erupt in jagged rocks, and the three struggled as their feet were ripped apart on the rocks. Ardán fell, was ripped apart, and died. Naoise put Deirdre on his shoulders and continued to move through the jagged rocks, but just as they reached the end of the rocky field, Naoise fell and also died.

King Conchobhar came and took Deirdre to his castle, saying, "You will marry me now." The next day, they buried Naoise. The King made Deirdre watch the burial to make her realize that that part of her life was over. As they dug the grave, Deirdre ran to the graveside and yelled, "Dig it deeper; dig it wider." Then she threw herself into the grave and died. The King would not let them be buried together. A grave was dug some distance apart.

Over the years, a yew tree grew from each grave. Eventually, the trees grew toward each other and became intertwined. The intertwined trees created a heart. There was such great outrage at Conchobhar's actions that people loyal to Naoise killed him. Two kings had died, Naoise who had been in line to be king, and King Conchobhar.

This is a tragic story about love and death. Naoise and his brothers faced death to save Deirdre. Deirdre fell into Naoise's grave, killing herself because she would not marry the King after he had killed the man she loved. Deirdre seemed fated for pain at birth from the druid's prophecy. But Deirdre had a nice life, filled with the beauty of the forest and a loving mate, a loyal family, his two brothers. Naoise died saving Dierdre, and she died being loyal to him by throwing herself into his grave. They could not have love in their earthly lives, but their love lived on, as the trees memorialized this.

Naoise and Dierdre's love inspired others to stay true. Sometimes in stories, there is death with no rebirth in the same life, but there is inspiration found in the reasons for the death. By facing adversity, vanquishing the tests, and accepting help, the transformation of the hero or heroine is carried on. Death in stories allows humans to accept death as part of life.

Chapter Twelve: The Storytelling Five

Storytelling Virtues Helix

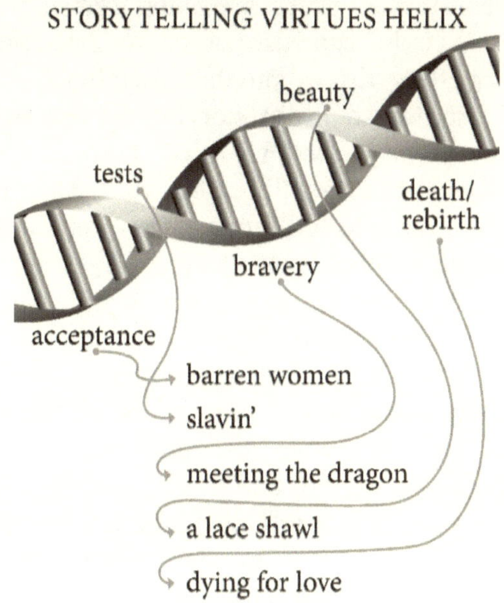

The DNA double helix structure gives instructions for survival and development, much like the storytelling virtues can guide humans towards their potential. The helix is not a linear structure but a spiral that weaves DNA's nucleotides together. The storytelling virtues of acceptance, tests, bravery, beauty and death/rebirth are like nucleotides. When embodied, they can move a human to wisdom and emotional strength. The virtues are interconnected, and a person can enter the helix at any point to weave their life together for wisdom.

In the storytelling helix above, acceptance comes from the story *The Children,* where parents needed to accept their duty to the Elder.

Tests are showcased in the story *Keep on Steppin.'* Dave suffered tests of slavery to finally be free. In the story *Sophia and Claude*, Sophia showed great bravery in taking the challenge to go meet the dragon, Claude, even though she could have died. In the story *The White Spider*, Pika's problem was solved by the beauty of the lace shawl woven by the spider. And *Deirdre*, in her story, actually died, rather than marry a King who had killed her lover and his brothers, created a symbol of love and toppling a king. The metaphor of the helix shows that these virtues are interlaced into a whole for transformation. People can use story to become whole and interweave storytelling virtues into their own lives.

Most stories showcase all the storytelling virtues—acceptance, tests, bravery, beauty, and death/rebirth. If humans foster these five virtues themselves, then they will become wise. As in Trungpa's definition of wisdom, people will emanate the qualities of softness, warmth, humor, and compassion. People's lives are story, and by seeing the patterns in storytelling wisdom, people can identify their lives as story and apply the storytelling virtues to navigate tests and make transcendent returns in the many cycles of life.

Looking at ups and downs as our life's story allows us to move into the liminal space of human wisdom. Seeing life as story gives us perspective, clarity, insight, and direction. By experiencing stories, we can see examples of embodying these virtues, and more importantly, we can open our eyes to how we are already embodying these virtues. I've saved some stories to further showcase the five virtues.

The Shaman Story

Most stories about shamans have life-threatening tests that often include the experience of dying and being reborn. Shamans have existed on all continents of the planet. Marcia Eliade's foundational book *The Way of the Shaman: Archaic Techniques of Ecstasy* documents shamanic practice in Russia. Of course, in the United States, most people think of shamans as those from American Indian tribes or the Inuit peoples in Alaska and Canada. The basic premise of a shaman is that a person in the community is called to be a shaman by extranormal, psychic experiences. The call is unavoidable and not initiated. Often, the person resists until they can no longer deny the reality of the experience. This person is then tested through many trials. Some report actual death before a rebirth happens. At that point, shamans can journey into altered realities to restore healing to their community.

In some shamanic journeying, the shaman travels to the sky or to the underground world through visions propelled by natural psychedelics or persistent drumbeats. Shamans' journeys are to heal their communities. Shamans often have spirit helpers who gift them a specific "way" to heal themselves and others. For example, the spirit helper of a bear might give a shaman strength. I personally see this metaphorically; each of us can use drumming or wilderness experiences to create altered states of consciousness to discover insight.

In this shaman story from Greenland, a young Inuit boy accepts the fact he has no future at his home, as his mother beats him with a sledge. His next test is to choose to become a shaman. He had already withstood the beatings from his mother. Then, on his path to be a shaman, he must rub a stone over the crack in the mountain over and over. As he does this, the spirit helpers come out of the crack. One is a bear that eats him. Bravery appears in the story as the would-be shaman faces these tests and comes back to meet his spirit helpers. Beauty also shows its face as one of his spirit helpers helps him catch salmon. Death and rebirth happen when he is reborn after the bear kills him.

- **Acceptance:** He must leave his abusive home, and he decides to become a shaman.
- **Tests:** His mother beats him. He must rub the rock on the stone over and over to listen to the voice coming up from the crack in the mountain. He has to face the spirit helpers coming out of the rock as well as a sea monster.
- **Bravery:** He faces pain and supernatural events.
- **Beauty:** A spirit helper in the form of a little man comes to help him catch salmon.

- **Death and Rebirth:** The boy died when the bear came out of the sea and ate him, and later he is reborn.

Let's look at the full story. A young Inuit boy made a sledge. After his mother beat him with it, he decided that he would become an *angakoq*, or shaman. The boy went to the mountain that faced the sunrise, where there was a very large crack in a granite ledge, high at the top of the mountain. He put a stone over the crack, then another on top of it. He rubbed the upper stone round against the lower in the direction that the sun moves. He did this until he could barely move his arms. He heard a voice calling him from beneath the earth. He didn't understand the words, and he was terrified. He decided that he would no longer eat entrails, livers, and hearts of seals, nor would he work in iron.

He went back the next day and rubbed the stone over and over in a circle. He heard the voice again and felt a violent pain. He did the same thing the next day, and this time the voice said, "Shall I come up?"

The boy said, "Yes, come up."

A huge sea monster came up and looked at the sunrise, then went back down. This is a spirit helper that the boy will work with when he becomes a shaman.

Winter came, and the boy did not go to the crack in the mountain. But in the spring, the boy repeated rubbing the stones, and a little man came up. This was his second spirit helper. He could catch salmon for the boy. The boy fainted after he saw the little man. When he awoke, the man was gone. The next spring, the boy went to a little lake. Another little man came up, his third spirit helper. The next year, the boy went to the ocean and threw a stone. An enormous bear came out and attacked him. He fainted and died. Then he came to. The boy had a bear and three spirits to help him when he grew up to be a shaman.

This story does not make logical sense. The boy was driven to be a shaman by an abusive mother, and he somehow knew that his journey started by rubbing a stone on another stone on a crack in a mountain. It was a frightening task. He heard supernatural voices and even experienced a monster. The task took many years, but through these tests, he received the gifts of three spirit helpers. Sometimes humans are drawn to do difficult things, and they don't really understand why. Out of a difficult journey sometimes comes a gift. A gift can be an ability, such as the strength to make a goal happen.

I have taught for many years at a graduate school for working adults, and it is a hard test. It can take up to six years to earn a PhD, often longer. Possibly, students could use the metaphor of the shaman experiencing tests and getting spirit helpers to help them through. Embodying the archetype of the shaman readies people to face tests and be open to seeing helpers. Tests pop up in life, and thinking as a shaman can help. Don't look for tests, but stay with the difficulty and be assured that gifts await if one accepts them. There is hope.

Xenophobe

I return again to my story *Xenophobe*, which embodies the storytelling virtues. As I made up the story, I wanted to use the imagery of (1) dragons, deep, powerful earth forces; (2) fire, tests through challenge; (3) flight, rising above the tests; and (4) the five-pointed star, a symbol of healing.

I learned about the symbolism of stars while presenting a workshop in an old Masonic building in downtown Prescott, Arizona. It had been converted into a bank, but the upper floor was rented for meetings, with a huge central room with transit windows and a star in the ceiling. I looked into Masonic symbology and learned that the star represented healing. In honor of the location of my workshop, I included the star in the story.

Recall, Xenophobe is a young dragon and the protagonist. He learns why his father died, to perform a ceremony to keep peace between the dragons and the humans. Xenophobe is selected to repeat this ceremony. He accepts that male dragons sacrifice themselves to keep peace with the humans. His test is to pretend to go through the sacrifice with the humans, but to break this cycle and create a new normal for peace. He is very brave to fly into outer space to retrieve a symbol of healing in a death-defying feat.

- **Acceptance:** Xenophobe realizes historically his role is to die, and he must deal with it.
- **Tests:** He must face the humans and rewrite the story.
- **Bravery:** He faces the humans and flies into space for the healing symbol of the star.
- **Beauty:** He catches the star in the sky, bringing back an awesome symbol for dragons and humans to move from violence to cooperation.
- **Death and Rebirth:** He faces the fact that he is supposed to die.

I chose *Xenophobe* to represent what people feared. Western society rests on patriarchy, the dominance of the strong to sustain the current order. It is not really about men but about power. Recall the Jungian analyst Marion Woodman, who proposed an emerging paradigm of androgyny in which humans have a sense of their spirituality and of their interconnection with other humans and nature as a value. I made Xenophobe a character of this emerging paradigm.

Xenophobe lived with his mother, Citron, in the mountains far away from humans. He spent beautiful days flying high over the rugged peaks. After his flights, he lay on a big granite slab by a pristine, mountain lake, warming languidly in the sun. Citron sometimes sunned by his side. Sometimes, Xenophobe watched her when she did not see him. He noticed that there was a deep sadness about her. One day, picking up on this sadness, a memory popped into his mind. It was of a huge ebony dragon that used to live with them. Insight dawned on him. "My dad," he thought. This gave him the strength to ask his mom, "Why are you sad?"

His mother looked at him and said, "Because dragons die."

More memories came back to him, those of his dad, named Ebony, being slaughtered by a small, upright animal with a knife. Through tears, he looked at his mother and asked, "But why do dragons die?"

His mother explained that there was a dance that dragons did with the little straight-up animals, called humans. Those animals lived in the valley below the dragons' rugged mountain caves, which had been chiseled out of granite. Periodically, a human came to the mouth of the cave at the base of the mountain, setting up a signal fire. A male dragon then flew down and pretended to fight, allowing the human to kill him. In this way, the dragon maintained peace in the world and protected the dragon village from humans.

As Xenophobe grew, he ruminated on this story, which did not seem right to him at all. He flew all over the mountains and sometimes spied on the human villages below. In his flights, he also met and fell in love with a golden female dragon called Halo. The two found their own cave in the dragons' mountain complex. They often visited Xenophobe's mother, Citron, and sunned beside her on the banks of the icy mountain lake above the tree line. Beside the lake were small bristlecone pine trees, tens of thousands of years old, that had been formed into gnarly shapes by the wind, hugging closely to the rock.

There came a time when it seemed Halo and Citron were pulling away from Xenophobe. He sensed that he would soon take his turn to face the human to represent the dragons in the deadly dance for peace. On the appointed day, led by an inner knowing, he flew out from his mountain cave and landed by the lake near the signal fire. He saw a tiny man with pieces of metal and a metal spike. He landed, and the man came at him. He knew he was to perform the dragon martyr role and pretend to fight, finally letting the human kill him. But Xenophobe had a different idea.

He put his big, clawed foot squarely on the human's chest, pushing him down and holding him there. He told the human, "We will break this cycle. No one has to die to keep peace. Climb on my back."

The human protested strongly but finally climbed on Xenophobe's back, and Xenophobe flew high through the clouds and higher above the atmosphere. The human was sorely afraid, but Xenophobe comforted him and told him to hold on tight. They were so high that the stars were nearby. He pointed at one star in particular. He told the human to reach out to the star. Again, the human was afraid, but Xenophobe urged him on. The human grabbed the star. It was so hot that it burned his hand, and he dropped it on the dragon's back, and it burned into the dragon's chest.

The dragon with the human on his back started spiraling back to the earth, exhaling fire at each turn. The dragons looked up from their mountain caves, and the humans looked up from their village. They were all struck with awe. No longer did human men need to kill dragons, and no longer did dragons need to pretend to be killed. They could live together in peace.

That is how the dragons broke the patriarchy. It was brave of Xenophobe to break the cycle of sacrifice, which included a pointless death. It was brave of the human to trust the dragon. It was brave of both of them to fly beyond the atmosphere and find a star.

Cupid and Psyche

Cupid and Psyche's story has the five storytelling virtues with an emphasis on beauty. This story tells of the perils of beauty, including jealousy and true love. There is no denial of the physical beauty of both Cupid and Psyche. Psyche accepts that she loves Cupid. She faces many challenges, but the main ones are Venus testing her to win the opportunity to be with Cupid. These tests included sorting different grains, getting the golden fleece, and even going to the underworld. She shows great bravery in going through these tests. The beauty in the story is physical as well as in the love and devotion Cupid and Psyche have for each other. Psyche dies and is reborn as an immortal.

- **Acceptance:** Psyche surrenders to her love for Cupid.
- **Tests:** The arrow designed to prompt Psyche to fall in love with a monster nicks Cupid who then falls in love with Psyche. Psyche's sisters tell her Cupid is a monster. Venus puts Psyche through tests.
- **Bravery:** Psyche and Cupid must be brave in the face of Venus to be together.
- **Beauty:** Psyche and Cupid are both exceptionally beautiful. After many tests, Psyche and Cupid realize they love each other.
- **Death and Rebirth:** The sisters die. Psyche dies but becomes immortal.

Physical beauty, as revealed by this story, can promote jealousy. The sisters die, and Venus loses her son. Psyche pays the ultimate price for her beauty by dying, but she becomes immortal through Cupid's true love. The wisdom of beauty in this story is that the beauty of love transcends all.

Now, let's look at the story in more detail. There was once a queen and king who had three beautiful daughters. One was particularly beautiful, and her name was Psyche. Her beauty was so great that all through the surrounding lands, people heard about her. It was said that she wasn't even a human. Rather, she was the goddess of beauty. People from all over brought her gifts and came to worship her and say their prayers to her. Psyche was unhappy, though. Her two sisters had married kings, but no one would dare ask Psyche to marry him because she seemed to be a goddess.

Venus heard of all this and was very angry, calling her son Cupid, the trickster god of love, to come to her. When Cupid's golden arrow struck someone with the slightest touch, that person or god fell in love with the next person seen. Because of this power, all the gods feared Cupid.

Venus said, "Cupid, you must help me. There is a woman, Psyche, who thinks she is as beautiful as me. We must teach her a lesson."

Cupid responded, "Great, I love to play tricks. What can I do for you, Mother?"

Venus directed him, "I want you to go to her when she is sleeping and prick her with your arrow so that she will fall madly in love with a monster that you show her."

Cupid raised his quill of arrows as he was leaving, "I'm on it, Mom." Cupid flew to Psyche's bedchamber as she was sleeping. He entered through a window and came close to her bed. As he leaned over and pulled his bow back, he hesitated, as he was struck by her beauty. She opened her eyes suddenly. Surprised, Cupid nicked himself with his arrow.

Cupid cried, "Oh no, I haven't fulfilled Mother's wishes!" And he flew away. Now he was madly in love with Psyche.

Psyche was so unhappy that she decided to consult an oracle, a god who could see into the future. She traveled to Delphi, where

Apollo, the oracle, lived. It was a hard trip up a large mountain. Psyche cried out when she saw the statue of Apollo, "Tell me, tell me, what will happen to me? Will I ever marry?"

Apollo spoke through his priestess. "You will wed, but it will be to someone who even the gods fear. Go to the top of the nearest mountain, and you will find out what will happen."

Psyche went home to say goodbye to her family. Everyone cried, but Psyche said, "Being married to a creature cannot be worse than living alone."

She climbed up the nearest mountain and stood waiting. She was afraid and shook a little as she stood there. All of a sudden, the warmth of Zephyrus, the gentle west wind, picked her up and carried her to the most beautiful castle she had ever seen.

Psyche walked in and exclaimed, "Wow, this is so amazing; it is so beautiful! But no one is here except me. It is like there is magic everywhere. When I sit down, there is food. If I reach out, someone pours me wine. There are clean and gorgeous clothes laid out for me. When I want to go to bed, the sheets are folded back for me. I love it here."

At dinner time, she went into the dining room, where all the lights were off except a few candles. Then she heard a voice, but she could not see who was talking. He was hiding in the darkness.

"Well, beautiful Psyche, welcome to my castle. We will meet each night for dinner and talk about our days. All your needs will be met. You must never see me, though. I want you to learn to love me for who I am, not how I look."

Psyche and the mysterious stranger started their life together, and Psyche began to love her life, but she missed her family. One night, Psyche pleaded, "Please, let my sisters come. I love you now, but I am alone so much, and I miss my family."

The mysterious man relented. "Well, if you must, you may let them come. But under no circumstances must you tell them about me. If you do, all will be lost."

The next morning, Psyche excitedly called Zephyrus. "Go, get my sisters as soon as possible." The sisters arrived. They were very impressed with the castle, and they pestered Psyche to find out about their host.

Finally, one sister said, "He is the creature whom everyone fears that Apollo said you would marry. You must go to his bedroom at night and kill him before he kills you."

Psyche didn't want to believe her sisters, but her fears took her over. She was often alone, and she longed to know her host. Finally, she lost control and decided to take a knife to her host's room. As she crept into his bedroom, she suddenly saw him. She was shocked!

He was not a monstrous creature but the handsome god Cupid. She reached out to touch an arrow in his quiver and pricked herself, falling immediately in love with him. However, he was so handsome and brilliant, and he had been so kind to her, that she would have fallen in love with him anyway.

Cupid startled. "What are you doing standing over me with a knife? Love cannot live without very strong trust. I am leaving you forever!"

Psyche was distraught and so ashamed that she had listened to her sisters' cruel doubts. Her sisters wanted to be with Cupid in the beautiful castle and went to the mountain to await the buoyancy of Zephyrus, the west wind, to take them to the wonderful castle. They jumped to let Zephyrus carry them, but he was not there, and they fell to their deaths.

Cupid flew to his mother with his pain, and being distraught and wanting to win Cupid back, Psyche went to Venus as well. Venus set up three tests for Psyche, assured that she would fail each one.

Venus directed Psyche: "You must sort this grain into three piles, one each of barley, wheat, and millet." Psyche began but was overwhelmed. Then she saw a group of ants and said, "Please help me, and I will share with you." The ants helped, and by sunset, all the grain was sorted. Venus didn't like this at all.

Venus gave Psyche her next test: "Now you must go out and find the golden sheep and bring me an armful of fleece."

Psyche thought this was easy. As she walked toward the sheep with golden fleece, she saw a sparrow that fell from its nest. She picked him up and saved him by returning him to his nest. The grateful mother sparrow said, "Don't try to gather the fleece now. The rams will kill you. Wait until midday when they go into the woods for shade. Then you can gather the golden fleece."

Psyche did just that, and she brought it to Venus, who was very peeved. "Okay, now I'll give you a test you cannot complete, you little arrogant snit. Take this box to Queen Proserpina in the land of the dead, so she can fill it with beauty. I need rejuvenation."

Cupid saw all this and finally realized that Psyche loved him. He knew it was a very dangerous task and was meant to kill Psyche. He came to her and gave her two gold coins and six honey cakes. He said, "Psyche, do not stop for any reason, and eat nothing. Tell no one you are from the land of the living. If you forget any of this, you will never return."

Psyche did as she was told. She gave the ferryman a gold coin to take her over the River Styx, which separated the living from the dead. She gave the three-headed dog, Cerberus, three honey cakes. She went to Proserpina and gave her the box and then received it back again. She ate nothing. On the way back, she gave the three-headed dog the last of the honey cakes and gave the ferryman the last coin. She returned to the land of the living. But she was tempted to open the box to have some of the beauty so that Cupid would love her. She opened it slowly, and then she fell as if she were dead.

Cupid flew to her, as he was waiting for her return. "Psyche, what have you done? I will kiss death from your lips and open your eyes." Psyche was revived, and Cupid flew her to meet Jupiter, the father of the gods. He made Psyche immortal, and she and Cupid lived as husband and wife forever. They had a daughter named Joy.

Coyote and the Cottontail: Cotton Tail Cheats Death

This Coyote story continues in a similar vein as the other Coyote stories, with the theme of being an anti-hero. *Coyote and the Cottontail* is found in *Coyote Stories,* published by the Navajo Curriculum Center of the Rough Rock Demonstration School. In this story, Coyote tries to trick people but ends up being tricked by himself. He flirts with death as he instigates mayhem with his animal cousins. Listeners laugh at Coyote's posture of arrogance as he falls from grace at the end of the story. People can identify with his failure and hubris, which is usually accompanied by a dash of humor. All survive, ready for the next test.

Coyote stories, of course, feature Coyote, but in this story, Cottontail is the protagonist, and he personifies the storytelling virtues. He accepts that he is trapped by Coyote in the rocks and further accepts that he will soon be Coyote's dinner. His test is to outwit Coyote by talking him out of methods to smoke Cottontail out of his hiding place. He is brave to stand up to Coyote and play tricks on him. It seems there is no way out, and that he must use his wits. Cottontail's ingenuity and agility are beautiful things. He faces death at Coyote's hand but eludes him.

- **Acceptance:** Cottontail accepts that he is trapped by Coyote.
- **Tests:** His tests are how to use his wits to trick Coyote out of killing him.
- **Bravery:** Cottontail is brave to not show fear when talking to Coyote.
- **Beauty:** Cottontail's escape is a vision of beauty.
- **Death and Rebirth:** Cottontail faces death but doesn't need to be reborn since he escapes.

In *Coyote and the Cottontail*, the story starts out with Coyote trotting along a wash, a dry streambed, feeling sorry for himself for not being able to catch a field mouse the previous day. This is a common state for Coyote—feeling sorry for himself. But he is indefatigable and bounces back to try each day. He sees a cottontail jump in front of him, spraying sand in his face. He catches Cottontail. Coyote is ready to eat the sweet little rabbit. However, Cottontail was not afraid. He was emboldened. He told Coyote he'd be sorry if he ate him right away; he said he had information that Coyote would like. Further, Cottontail said, "I'm old and tough and not very tasty." He exhorts Coyote to take his claws from his neck so that they can talk.

Cottontail told Coyote that men hunt animals like him with bows and arrows. He demonstrated how he could leap away just before the bow zings. Cottontail said, "Let me show you."

At that moment, Cottontail jumped away and hid in a crevice amid a pile of stones. Coyote said, "I'll get you out." He went to get cedar bark to smoke Cottontail out.

Cottontail said, "You can't waste cedar bark. That is my food."

Then Coyote responded, "Okay, I'll get sagebrush." But then Cottontail repeated his criticism.

Finally, Coyote said, "I'll get pitch." Then he used his magical power to start the fire. Black smoke billowed at the opening to the rock pile.

Cottontail said, "Blow harder." Coyote did, and there was so much black smoke from the fire that his vision became clouded. At that point, Cottontail pushed the rocks away and leaped to freedom.

At the end of the story, Cottontail eluded death, and Coyote stayed hungry. Both faced tests of the story. Coyote didn't get a meal. Cottontail got away. Cottontail outsmarted Coyote, and instead of dying as a Coyote meal, he jumped away. Cottontail gained confidence and continued his life after using his wits against Coyote.

Epilogue: Life as Story

As John Lennon said, "Life doesn't imitate art; life is art." It is the same for story. Story is not about life. Story is life. When people use storytelling virtues and the storytelling cycle as patterns in their lives to gain perspective, clarity, and direction, they grow in wisdom.

My definition of wisdom documented earlier integrates ideas from Thomas Aquinas's lifeability, making one's life work, and from Chögyam Trungpa's transformation of the inner being to warmth, softness, humor, and compassion. This may seem odd to draw from a Christian and a Buddhist scholar to define wisdom, but these are two great traditions that grapple with understanding the human condition. I'm interested in wisdom not from a religious perspective but from a human development viewpoint. What I had put together from Trungpa's work was what I might call a transformed being. A person's inner being had actually changed—not only a changed topography of the mind but also a changed topography of the mind-body. Trungpa's words mention spaciousness filled with humor and friendliness as well as the embodiment of compassion. Therefore, wisdom is not what a person knows but what a person is. The transformation fosters Aquinas's lifeability, making one's life amid the stream of wisdom.

The storytelling virtues of acceptance, tests, bravery, beauty, and death/rebirth can be embodied by moving an everyday difficulty into the mythic realm by using the simple story structure. The difficult situation becomes a test in the storytelling cycle. Finding an archetype that could be an alter ego moves our lives into the mythic realm. In this realm, we tap the collective unconscious, and the patterns humans have laid down since ancient times about how to navigate adversity. As the story emerges, and we embody the main characteristic, be it strength or cleverness, we gain perspective of the situation. The perspective quiets the emotional response to the situation. Also using the storytelling cycle, we can look for tests to helpers, either people around, inner characteristics, values, or insight to transform our awareness. A return might be to defuse the situation, to see how we might have handled it differently, or find solace in some other way.

It is important to be playful and imaginative, almost like we are creating a movie script. Being playful allows the mind to relax, so inner resources can be activated to transform a difficult situation into a situation of strength.

When hearing or telling a story, we move into spaces to join with human stories across time. As an ancient human technology to pass on culture, values, and patterns to survive and thrive in adversity, humans naturally move through a threshold—or liminal space—that holds this wisdom. Over the years, I've taken the storytelling cycle to help people move difficult times in their lives into the mythic realm to find their inner knowing connected to the tapestry of human wisdom.

You might want to take a liminal turn and move an experience to the storytelling realm. The idea is to be playful as you make up your story. Let your imagination go. It is similar to brainstorming. No idea is too silly or outrageous. True, when dealing with tests in life, it is serious business, but the conscious mind relaxes and opens when thinking outside the box and being divergent.

Find and Name Your Test

Think about a time in the recent past when something happened that you didn't like or about a situation you were in that didn't feel good. Take a few minutes to get quiet, a breath or two, uncross your legs, and settle into your body. See the situation in your mind's eye as if it is happening again, as if you are watching a movie. Use all the senses—what do you see and hear, touch and smell and taste? Do you move in the setting? Notice the surroundings, furniture, or surfaces. If you're outside, notice plants, grass, or the sky. Find where you feel strongest in your body—your stomach, head, or chest. Once you have a good sense of the imagery and the concomitant emotions of this situation, you can put a name to your test.

Find and Name Your Archetype

The next step is to find an archetype. This is the main character of the story who conveys a specific characteristic. This imaginary character, or your alter ego, will go through the same test you have experienced. Select the type of your character and the characteristic you think it represents. Characteristics don't need to be just the good ones. Recall paradoxical thinking as part of wisdom. Sometimes you need to be weak to be strong. Sometimes embodying vulnerability will open your eyes to see new things.

Archetypes and Characteristics

Example of Archetypes	Example of Characteristics
hero	brave
priest	inquisitive
princess	curious
monster	deep
prince	wounded
queen	caring
artist	musical
painter	open
movie star	knowledgeable
handsome boy	innocent
father	wise
fool	vulnerable
magician	insecure
elder	loving
warrior	creative
priestess	afraid
wizard	angry
learner	wondering
king	foolish
scholar	trusting
musician	loving

writer	beautiful
beauty	ugly
mother	strong
teacher	powerful
rebel	weak
child	lazy
wise person	hardworking
others, as you imagine	others, as you imagine

After choosing a type and the characteristic that you think matches you, name your main character and select a color that you think goes with this character. Colors and rich sensory description are a given in story, and using them will move you faster into the mythic realm.

Find and Name Your Helpers

As you start imagining your main character with a type, characteristic, name, and color, you can imagine the helpers who will aid in the navigation through the tests. Helpers can be the characteristic you've chosen for your main character. They can be friends, relatives, or strangers who happen along. They might be animals, magical creatures, deities, or relatives who have passed.

Visualize the Beginning

The preparation for the story and the stage are almost set. Imagine the beginning. What would the beginning be like, the setting? Is it inside or outside? What are the colors? What is the character wearing? Think of it as setting the opening scene in a novel or the set design of a play.

Think About the Return

Sometimes the return will come spontaneously as one starts telling the story. Insight comes from merging with the mythic realm as the story emerges from the teller. This is a lot like improvisational work; the form emerges as the work progresses. Therefore, if nothing comes to mind, the story can begin and take its own form.

Tell Your Story

The elements are all there, and the cycle is almost complete except for the return. Begin with the first scene, add the test, bring in the helpers, and see what comes.

I recently held a workshop for graduate students titled *Storytelling and Wisdom*. I took them through the cycle with the steps, and wow, they created brilliant stories! Insight, strength, healing, and awareness all emerged.

As this book comes to an end, as all good stories must, I encourage you now to tell your story.

Tell a story from the heart
Hear a story of joy
Tell a story of pain, joy, clarity, or confusion
Hear a story that inspires
Tell a story of the past, the in between, and the future
Where you came from, where you are going
Open the pain, mend the mind
Touch the human spirit
Tell a story
    to be wild
    to be true
    to be you
Tell a story
    to heal a wound
    to find a way
    to walk with truth
Tell a story
    with an open heart
    with a ruptured mind
    and a body in sync
Tell your story, which is my story, their story, the human story
Tell a story

    for now
    for then
    for beyond
Hear a story, yes, hear a story
Hear a story so others may know that they are heard
Tell a story for the work as Gaia lives and breathes the Earth
The Earth has no tongue
Tell her story so you can tell all stories
Story now, story true, story here and far, story yours, mine, theirs
Blanche, noir, rouge, jaune, bruin
Stories throughout and within
Sing

A Note about References and Cultural Competency & Humility

Format for References and Citations

To make the book accessible, I did not use in-text citations for concepts from references. Authors are mentioned, as well as book titles, at times. These authors and books are listed in the bibliography alphabetically. Quotes are accompanied by the author's name, and the references for the quotes can be found in the bibliography.

Cultural Competence and Cultural Humility

First off, I want to say that I am in the process of becoming more culturally competent. It is not a state one achieves. Using the trite but true Carl Rogers' quote, finding cultural competence is a journey, not a destination. I can say that I aspire to be culturally competent and to have cultural humility. My journey has been a long one and continues. Let me remind you of some of the key point when I was developing my cultural competency.

Growing up in Kansas City, Missouri, in the 60s, civil rights were very much a part of my family and my religious life. As a graduate student, I worked as an educational consultant in the urban school districts of the Bronx, Philadelphia, and Indianapolis, and on the Hopi and the Northern Cheyenne Nations. I started a program for American Indian teacher aides to earn their credentials. During this work, I learned that my Western Eurocentric cultural educational training was culturally laden. This learning was that, instead of hierarchies, problem-solving, and individual achievement, I needed to learn about cycles, stories, and listening.

Teaching as a Fulbright professor in a village near Anand, Gujarat, India, I learned that I didn't know that much about cultural competence and learned that I needed to start by finding out about my own culture and, with respect, create a beginner's mind for other cultures. These experiences have sensitized me to cultural appropriation. When I started studying wheels, sometimes known as medicine wheels, as an organizing tool for information and as a way to create balance and harmony in an endeavor, I examined my motivation. Wheels might be considered a concept from indigenous North American tribes. However, the more I studied wheels, I found them all over the world from ancient times. I found a wheel in Scotland that ancient kings used to visit their lands; a wheel in Gandhi's ashram in Ahmedabad, India, to show how to create a just, civil society; a wheel in Africa used by spiritual leaders for ceremonies. Wheels are a part of human history across the planet. As with the wheel, stories have been used by the peoples of the earth since ancient times. All people can find a cultural story that their ancestors told under the stars from ancient times. Humans across all cultures partake in the storytelling tradition.

Sources for the Book's Stories

The vast majority of the stories I've shared in this book were passed down in the oral tradition before they were set in the written word. Once in word form, they were adapted by many other storytellers and researched and commented upon by scholars. Some stories are referred to multiple times to show different dimensions of the storytelling virtues.

Here I share with you suggested sources for the stories if you want to read more about them.

(Note: Some of the stories are from indigenous North American people. Throughout the book, I use American Indian, Native American, and indigenous, all accepted terms used by indigenous North American people. If an author uses a specific tribal name, I use that.

Avalokiteshvara, Wang, Michelle C. "Thousand-Armed and Thousand-Eyed Avalokiteshvara." *Conversations: An Online Journal of the Center for the Study of Material and Visual Cultures of Religion* (2014).

Buffalo Woman, Goble, Paul. *Buffalo Woman.* Aladdin Books, Macmillan Publishing Company, 1984

Cinderlad, Literature Committee. *Told Under the Green Umbrella: Old Stories for New Children.* The McMillan Company. 1939.

Coyote and His Pups, original by the author

Coyote and the Cottontail, Rosessel, Robert, A. and Dillon Platero, editors. *Coyote Stories.* Navaho Curriculum Center. Rough Rock Demonstration School. Diné Inc.,1968.

Cupid and Psyche, Craft, Marie Charlotte. *Cupid and Psyche.* William Morrow and Company, Inc. 1996.

Deirdre, Stephens, James. *Deirdre.* New York Macmillan 1923.

Gaia, Olson, Carl. The Book of the Goddess, Past and Present: An Introduction to Her Religion. The Crossroad Publishing Company, 1994.

Ganesha, Grewal, Royina. *The Book of Ganesha.* Penguin Books India, 2009.

Isis, Olson, Carl. The Book of the Goddess, Past and Present: An Introduction to Her Religion. The Crossroad Publishing Company. 1994.

John the True, Literature Committee. *Told Under the Green Umbrella: Old Stories for New Children.* The Macmillan Company, 1942.

Juan Bobo, Barlow, Genevieve. *Leyendes Lationo-Americanas.* National Textbook Company. 1991.

Keep on Steppin', Lester, Julius. *Black Folktales.* Richard W Baron, 1969.

La Llorona, Perez, Domino Renee. *There Was a Woman: La Llorona from Folklore to Popular Culture.* University of Texas Press, 2008.

Lilith, Olson, Carl. The Book of the Goddess, Past and Present: An Introduction to Her Religion. The Crossroad Publishing Company. 1994.

Ramayana, Nagra, Daljit. *Ramayana*. Faber & Faber, 2013.
Sophia, Schaup, Susanne. Sophia: Aspects of the Divine Feminine Past and Present. Nicolas-Hays.1997.
Sophia and Claude, original story by the author
The Blind Men and the Elephant, Saxe, John G. *The Blind Men and the Elephant*. Enrich Spot Limited, 2016.
The Children, Omoleye, Amoke. *Yoruba Children's Tales*. Amoke Omoleye Pub, 1990.
The Dragon's Robe, Lattimore, Deborah Nourse. *The Dragon's Robe*. Harper Collins, 1990.
The Four Directions, original story, adapted from an oral story told by Wil Numkena.
The Shaman Story, Halifax, Joan. *Shamanic Voices*. E.P. Dutton, 1979.
The White Spider, Barlow, Genevieve. *The White Spider's Gift. Latin American Tales*. McNally & Company, 1966.
Xenophobe, original story by the author

Bibliography

Achterberg, Jeanne. *Imagery in Healing: Shamanism and Modern Medicine*. Shambhala Publications, 2002.

Allen, Paula Gunn. *The Sacred Hoop: Recovering the Feminine in American Indian Traditions*. Beacon Press, 1992.

Ansbacher, Heinz L. "Adler's Interpretation of Early Recollections: Historical Account." *Journal of Individual Psychology,* 29.2, 1973, 135.

Balmer, D. H., E. Gikundi, and C. O. Rachier. "The Evaluation of an Adolescent Programme Based Upon a Narrative Story, Role Plays and Group Discussion in Kenya." *Journal of Psychology in Africa,* 12.2, 2002, 101-118.

Baltes, Paul B., and Ursula M. Staudinger. "Wisdom: A Metaheuristic (Pragmatic) to Orchestrate Mind and Virtue Toward Excellence." *American Psychologist,* 55.1, 2000, 122.

Barlow, Genevieve. *Leyendes Lationo-Americanas*. National Textbook Company, 1991.

Barlow, Genevieve. *The White Spider's Gift. Latin American Tales*. McNally & Company, 1966.

Benally, Herbert John. "Diné Philosophy of Learning." *Journal of Navajo Education,* 6.1, 1988, 10–13.

Bronfenbrenner, Urie. *Ecological Systems Theory*. Jessica Kingsley Publishers, 1992.

Bryant, Edwin F. *The Yoga Sutras of Patanjali: A New Edition, Translation, and Commentary*. North Point Press, 2015.

Cady, Susan, Ronan, Marion & Taussig, Hall, *Sophia: The Future of Feminist Spirituality*. Winston Pr, 1996.

Cajete, Gregory A. "Children, Myth and Storytelling: An Indigenous Perspective." *Global Studies of Childhood.* 7.2, 2017, 113-130.

Campbell, Joseph. *The Hero with a Thousand Faces*. Vol. 17, New World Library, 2008.

Craft, Marie Charlotte. *Cupid and Psyche*. William Morrow and Company, Inc. 1996.

Dass, Ram. *Be Here Now*. Harmony, 2010.

Dass, Ram. *The Only Dance There Is*. Anchor, 2011.

Edinger, Edward F. *Ego and Archetype*. Shambhala Publications, 2017.

Edlich, Richard F., and Kübler-Ross, Elisabeth. "On Death and Dying in the Emergency Department." *The Journal of Emergency Medicine,* 10.2, 1992, 225–229.

Eliade, Mircea. *Shamanism: Archaic Techniques of Ecstasy*, Vol. 76, Princeton University Press, 2020.

Elms, Alan C. "Apocryphal Freud: Sigmund Freud's Most Famous "Quotations" and Their Actual Sources." *Annual Psychoanalysis*, 29, 2001, 83–104.

Estés, Clarissa Pinkola. *Women Who Run with the Wolves: Myths and Stories of the Wild Woman*. Ballantine, 1992.

Folan, Lilias M. *Lilias Yoga and You*. Bantam Books, 1976.

Garcia, Kenneth. *The Pursuit of Intellectual and Spiritual Wholeness, 1920–1960. In Academic Freedom and the Telos of the Catholic University*. Palgrave Macmillan. New York, 2012.

Gawain, Shakti. *Creative Visualization: Use the Power of Your Imagination to Create What You Want in Your Life*. New World Library, 2016.

Green, Elmer, and Alyce Green. "General and Specific Applications of Thermal Biofeedback." *Subtle Energies & Energy Medicine Journal Archives,* 10.1, 1979.

Goble, Paul. *Buffalo Woman*. Aladin Books, Macmillan Publishing Company, 1984.

Harner, Michael J., Mishlove, Jeffrey, and Bloch, Arthur. *The Way of the Shaman*. Harper & Row, 1990.

Hartelius, G., Caplan, M., and M. A. Rardin. "Transpersonal Psychology: Defining the Past, Divining the Future." *The Humanistic Psychologist,* 35(2), 2007,135–160.

Isaksen, Scott G., Mary C. Murdock, and Roger L. Firestien. *The Emergence of a Discipline: Understanding and Recognizing Creativity*, Vol. 1, Greenwood Publishing Group, 1993.

Iyengar, Bellur Krishnamukar Sundara. *Light on the Yoga Sutras of Patañjali*. Aquarian/Thorsons, 1993.

Iyengar, Bellur Krishnamukar Sundara, and Yehudi Menuhin. *Light on Yoga: Yoga Dipika*. Aquarian/Thorsons, 1968.

Jakobsh, Doris. "3HO/Sikh Dharma of the Western Hemisphere: The 'Forgotten' New Religious Movement?" *Religion Compass*, 2.3, 2008, 385–408.

Jung, Carl Gustav. *The Collected Works of C.G. Jung*. No. 20. Bollingen Foundation, 1953.

Kaufmann, Geir. "What to Measure? A New Look at the Concept of Creativity." *Scandinavian Journal of Educational Research*, 47(3), 2003, 235–251.

Kegan, Robert. *In Over Our Heads: The Mental Demands of Modern Life*. Harvard University Press, 1994.

Lancaster, B. L. & Palframan, J. T. "Coping with Major Life Events: The Role of Spirituality and Self-Transformation." *Mental Health, Religion & Culture*, 12 (3), 2009, 257–276.

Lao Tzu, Li Er. *Tao Te Ching*. Wordsworth, 1997.

Lasater, Judith Hanson. *Relax and Renew: Restful Yoga for Stressful Times*. Shambhala Publications, 2016.

Lattimore, Deborah Nourse. *The Dragon's Robe*. Harper Collins, 1990.

Lester, Julius. *Keep on Steppin' Black Folktales*. Richard W Baron, 1969.

Literature Committee. *Told Under the Green Umbrella: Old Stories for New Children*. The Macmillan Company, 1942.

Macy, Joanna. *Greening of the Self*. Parallax Press, 2013.

Macy, Joanna. *World as Lover, World as Self: Courage for Global Justice and Ecological Renewal*. Parallax Press, 2003.

Marks, David F. "Visual Imagery Differences in the Recall of Pictures." *British Journal of Psychology*, 6.4, 1973, 17–24.

Maslow, Abraham H. *Toward a Psychology of Being*. Simon and Schuster, 2013.

McGivney, Annette. *Pure Land: A True Story of Three Lives, Three Cultures and the Search for Heaven on Earth.* AUX Media, 2017.

Mellon, Nancy. *Storytelling & the Art of Imagination.* Harper Element, 1992.

Murdock, Mary C. "The Emergence of a Discipline: Issues and Approaches to the Study of Creativity." *The Emergence of a Discipline: Understanding and Recognizing Creativity,* 1, 1993, 13.

Nelson, Annabelle. *Living the Wheel: Working with Emotions, Terror and Bliss with Imagery.* York Beach, Maine: Samuel Weiser, Inc., 1993.

Nelson, Annabelle. *Storytelling PowerBook.* The WHEEL Council, 1997.

Nelson, Annabelle. *The Learning Wheel: Holistic and Multicultural Lesson Planning.* Zephyr Press and The WHEEL Council, 1998.

Nelson, Annabelle. "The Spacious Mind: Using Archetypes for Transformation Towards Wisdom." *The Humanistic Psychologist,* 35, 2007, 235–246.

Nelson, Annabelle. *Archetypal Imagery and the Spirit Self: Techniques for Coaches and Therapists.* Jessica Kingsley Publishers, 2014.

Nelson, Annabelle and Bisi Lalemi. "The Role of Imagery Training on Tohono O'odham Children's Creativity Scores." *Journal of American Indian Education,* May 1991, 24–32.

Nelson, Annabelle, and Brian Arthur. "Decreasing At-Risk Youth's Alcohol and Marijuana Use. *Journal of Primary Prevention,* 24:2, 2003, 169–180.

Nelson, Annabelle, David Cordova, Andrew S Walters, and Elsie Szecsy. "Storytelling for Empowerment for Latino Teens: Increasing HIV Prevention Knowledge and Attitudes." *Journal of Adolescent Research,* 31.2, 2016, 202–231.

Nelson, Annabelle, Charles McClintock, Anita Perez-Ferguson, Mary Nash Shawver, and Greg Thompson. "Storytelling Narratives: Social Bonding as Key for Youth At-Risk." *Child & Youth Care Forum,* 37 (3), 2008, 127–137.

Nelson, Annabelle, Orlando, Carolyn, and Murphy, Nola. *HIV Storybook, Science, Risk Factor Relationships & Self- Efficacy.* The WHEEL Council, 2003.

Nelson-Burford, Annabelle. *How to Focus the Distractable Child.* R & E Publications, 1985.

Nelson-Burford, Annabelle. "Imagery's Physiological Base". *Journal of the Society for Accelerative Learning and Teaching,* 13 (4), 1989, 363–373.

Omoleye, Amoke. *Yoruba Children's Tales.* Amoke Omoleye Pub, 1990.

Olson, Carl. *The Book of the Goddess, Past and Present: An Introduction to Her Religion.* The Crossroad Publishing Company.1994.

Palamos, Karen. "Nature, Human Ecopsychological Consciousness and the Evolution of Paradigm Change in the Face of Current Ecological Crisis." *International Journal of Transpersonal Studies,* 35.2, 2016.

Pinker, Steven. *The Better Angels of Our Nature: Why Violence Has Declined.* Penguin Books, 2012.

Perls, Frederick S., and John O. Stevens. "Gestalt Therapy Verbatim." 1969.

Pert, Candace B. *Molecules of Emotion: The Science Behind Mind-Body Medicine.* Simon and Schuster, 2010.

Piaget, Jean. *The Language and Thought of the Child,* Vol. 10. Psychology Press, 2002.

Piaget, Jean and Bärbel Inhelder. *The Psychology of the Child.* Basic Books, 2008.

Pribram, Karl H. *Languages of the Brain: Experimental Paradoxes and Principles in Neuropsychology.* Prentice-Hall, 1971.

Rama, Swami, Rudolph Ballentine, and Swami Ajaya. *Yoga and Psychotherapy: The Evolution of Consciousness.* Himalayan Institute Press, 1976.

Restak, Richard and Grubin, David. *The Secret Life of the Brain.* Joseph Henry Press, 2001.

Roessel Jr., Robert A. & Dillon Platero, editors. *Coyote Stories.* Navaho Curriculum Center. Rough Rock Demonstration School. Diné Inc., 1968.

Rogers, Carl Ransom and Kramer, Peter D. *On Becoming a Person: A Therapist's View of Psychotherapy*. Houghton Mifflin Harcourt, 1995.

Saxe, John G. *The Blind Men and the Elephant*. Enrich Spot Limited, 2016.

Schaup, Susanne. *Sophia: Aspects of the Divine Feminine Past and Present*. Nicolas-Hays, 1997.

Sheldrake, Rupert. *New Science of Life*. Icon Books Ltd, 2005.

Singh, Manvir. "The Cultural Evolution of Shamanism." *Behavioral and Brain Sciences*, 41, 2018.

Smith, Huston. *The Religions of Man*. Ishi Press, 1958.

Springer, Sally P. and Deutsch, Georg. *Left Brain Right Brain*. W. H. Freeman, 1981.

Stenner, Paul. *Liminality and Experience: A Transdisciplinary Approach to the Psychosocial. Studies in the Psychosocial (STIP)*. Palgrave Macmillan, 2017.

Stephens, James. *Deirdre*. New York Macmillan 1923.

Storm, Hyemeyohsts. *Seven Arrows*. Ballantine Books, 1972.

Sugihara, Megumi. "How to Love, Care, and Make a Difference: Non-Dual Global Justice in Action." Diss. Fielding Graduate University, 2015.

Suzuki, Shunryu. *Zen Mind, Beginner's Mind*. Shambhala Publications, 2020.

Tafoya, Terry. "Coyote's Eyes: Native Cognition Styles." *Journal of American Indian Education*, 1981, 21–33.

Tedeschi, Richard G. and Calhoun, Lawrence G. "Posttraumatic Growth: Conceptual Foundations and Empirical Evidence." *Psychological Inquiry*, 15, 2004, 1–18.

Thornton, Russell. *American Indian Holocaust and Survival: A Population History Since 1492*. University of Oklahoma Press, 1967.

Torrance, E. Paul and Michael F. Shaughnessy. "An Interview with E. Paul Torrance: about Creativity." *Educational Psychology Review*, 1998, 441–452.

Trungpa, Chögyam. *The Heart of the Buddha: Entering the Tibetan Buddhist Path, Vol. 1*. Shambhala, 1991.

Vivekananda, Swami. *Raja Yoga*. Advaita Ashrama: Mayawati, Champawat, Himalayas, Kolkata. 2003.

Van Gennep, Arnold. *The Rites of Passage*. University of Chicago Press, 2019.

von Franz, Marie-Louise. *Aurora Consurgens*. Princeton University Press, 1985.

Walsh, Roger. "The Varieties of Wisdom: Contemplative, Cross-cultural, and Integral Contributions." *Research in Human Development*, 8.2, 2011, 109–127.

Woodman, Marion. *The Ravaged Bridegroom: Masculinity in Women*, Vol. 41. Inner City Books, 1990.

Woodman, Marion and Dickson, Elinor. *Dancing in the Flames: The Dark Goddess in the Transformation of Consciousness*. Shambhala Publications, 1996.